ALL HANDS ON DECK

How U.S. Navy Submariners Structure, Systemize, & Optimize for Success

Jeff Barnes

ALL HANDS ON DECK: HOW U.S. NAVY SUBMARINERS STRUCTURE, SYSTEMIZE, & OPTIMIZE FOR SUCCESS

Copyright © 2018 by Jeff Barnes.

All rights reserved. No part of this book may be reproduced or transmitted in any form or by any means without written permission from the author.

ISBN: 978-1720557562

The Most Amazing Opportunity You'll Get Today!

Get it All for Just $1!

This book, although amazing and fun (in my humble opinion), is not complete without the accompanying resources in store for you online. I have taken the time to provide you with additional tools, resources, work books, and even some audio interviews I've conducted with others over the years to help you scale your business faster and with greater certainty.

The goal of this book and its bonuses is to help you scale your business using the right strategies coupled with the right systems, allowing you to make a greater positive impact in this world. By purchasing this book, whether the e-book, audiobook, or physical print copy, you are entitled to receive all these incredible resources *for just $1* by simply visiting the webpage listed below.

It is my sincere hope that you will take me up on this offer and grab your resources today. After all, some of the strategies listed inside these two covers could get me blacklisted and the website shut down!* So be sure to grab your bonuses today!

Since this book was first released, I took over the role of CEO at Angel Investors Network and have moved all our resources over there. Now you can access our Inner Circle and get access to over 100 hours of additional training on how to start, scale, and eventually sell or exit your business.

---

* Okay, maybe they won't get me shut down, but you never know!

At Angel Investors Network we are helping you create wealth and abundance through the power of Angel Investing & Entrepreneurship.

All Hands on Deck is a great complement to the resources we have available online, and now you can access everything starting at just one dollar!

To get access to these incredible resources, including live training, workbooks, and more, simply visit www.AngelNetwork.com/Bonus.

GO TO
WWW.ANGELNETWORK.COM/BONUS TO
GET STARTED TODAY!

Similar Books to Read

If you are at all like me, then you appreciate recommendations for good books that are in line with the genre/category of the book you're reading. This is how I built up my arsenal of information—by following the breadcrumbs of what authors I follow also read. Instead of putting it at the back like most, I'll list it up front so you don't forget!

1. *No B.S. Direct Marketing* by Dan S. Kennedy.
   This book quite literally changed the way I look at building a business completely from the ground up and has caused a major paradigm shift for myself and countless others.

2. *Extreme Ownership* by Jocko Willink and Leif Babin.
   An incredible read from two former U.S. Navy SEALs outlining leadership and strategies from the world's most elite fighting unit.

3. *Outwitting the Devil* and *Own Your Own Mind* by Napoleon Hill.
   Yes, everyone recommends Hill's *Think and Grow Rich* as a cornerstone for their success, but in my opinion, these two volumes are much more insightful and helpful as they relate to how to use your mind to think!

4. *Relentless* by Tim S. Grover.
   Tim describes the mind and makeup of superstars like Dwayne Wade and Michael Jordan and gives you permission to be okay with demanding more of yourself and those around you.

5. *Drive* by Daniel H. Pink.
   If you are building a team, then you must know how to properly motivate them. If you fail at this, you fail at running a business.

6. *Start with Why* by Simon Sinek.
   Simon helps us understand what drives us to follow certain dreams and helps us find fulfillment by understanding where our ambitions originate.

7. *Ready, Fire, Aim* by Michael Masterson (aka Mark Ford).
   Don't delay getting started because it isn't perfect…just start!

8. *Traction* by Gino Wickman.
   As I read this book, I couldn't help but think I'd written parts of it myself as Wickman's thoughts and ideas on how to properly structure a business very much mirror my own. This is a very well laid out guide on how to get traction in your business.

9. *Deep Work* by Jeff Bottoms.
   I finished the book in your hands in about three months total, which was slow by my account. Most people take years to accomplish very little because they can't actually focus and get shit done. This book tells you how to do that.

10. *The One Thing* by Gary Keller.
    If someone builds a billion-dollar business from scratch, you should perk up and listen. Gary Keller of Keller-Williams Realty has done just that and outlines a big part of his success in this book.

11. *The Ultimate Sales Machine* by Chet Holmes.
    The late Chet Holmes had a significant hand in helping Tony Robbins become the powerhouse he is today, and he did that through understanding how to motivate people to buy.

12. *The Millionaire Maker: Act, Think, and Make Money the Way the Wealthy Do* by Loral Langemeier.
    Loral has been my mentor for many years, and this book outlines the principles and strategies of starting and growing your business if you want to earn like the wealthiest 1 percent

Table of Contents

Disclaimer i
Introduction 1
Background 7
An Oath 9
Chapter One: The Best Laid Plans 13
Chapter Two: Captain You? 21
Chapter Three: Damn the Torpedoes! 25
Chapter Four: Leading with Systems 35
Chapter Five: Critical Operations 41
Chapter Six: Marketing & Sales Uranium 47
Chapter Seven: Operation: Customer Service Excellence 53
Chapter Eight: Streamlining Service Delivery 61
Chapter Nine: Eliminate Waste 63
Chapter Ten: Enhance the Customer Experience 65
Chapter Eleven: Provide Meaningful Feedback 67
Chapter Twelve: Create a Procedure 71
Chapter Thirteen: Make It Repeatable 81
Chapter Fourteen: Make It Scalable 83
Chapter Fifteen: Move the Expertise Upstream 87
Chapter Sixteen: Efficient Organization 91
Chapter Seventeen: Whiskey Tango Foxtrot! 99
Chapter Eighteen: Optimize, Innovate, Transform 109
Chapter Nineteen: The Key Ingredient 119
Chapter Twenty: Owning Your Role 127
Chapter Twenty-One: Putting It All Together 143
Chapter Twenty-Two: Startup, Innovate, Operate 149

Chapter Twenty-Three: Optimize & Innovate 153
Chapter Twenty-Four: Conclusion 161
Appendix One: Nine Nuclear Navy Principles 163
Appendix Two: Resources 171
Appendix Three: Coaching 175
Appendix Four: Speaking 177
Appendix Five: Consulting 179
Glossary & Terms 181
Bibliography 209
About the Author 211

Acknowledgments

To My Parents.
Even when you didn't think we noticed, we always saw how hard you both worked, and whether by accident or design, it worked. Words can't express my gratitude.

To My Grandparents.
For somehow surviving the worst atrocities mankind has seen and still coming out with the best attitudes and personality any kid could hope for. I still laugh from our memories.
I miss you.

Disclaimer

I had a football coach in middle school who was a Vietnam Veteran. He had a quick wit and a sharp tongue, and he made sure all of us on the team knew he meant business. He didn't mince words.

Later, Dan "Dirt" Enewold was an algebra and geometry teacher for me throughout high school and coached the high school baseball team for a short time while I was there. I appreciated his hard-nosed, no-nonsense way of getting things done, both on the field and in the classroom. Many others may have preferred a "softer, gentler" approach to sports and learning, but I was one of the few who truly enjoyed Dan's approach.

He had a saying for a few of us, one that I feel fit very well. He'd say, "Barnes, you are one rude, crude, and obscene dude!"[1] I'm sure this is a saying he used back in the Vietnam days with his Army brothers, but it stuck with me for all this time.

This book continues Dan's tradition of staying as close to the truth as possible without mincing words. My accounts are full of phrases and euphemisms that might make you cringe, blush, or furious. Any way, it is how I recall what occurred, and for that I make no apologies.

We are submariners, and we can cuss like the best of them. I didn't want to deny you of our rich history or ridiculous anecdotes and stories. You might be enticed to write a nasty review of my foul language and terse tone or think I'm just a plain old bad guy because of how this book is written. That's your choice, but I'd suggest you read the whole book before you make that decision.

---

1. Not much has changed. I'm slightly more refined, but sometimes that's like putting lipstick on a pig. It ain't always pretty in this book, but it can be fun and incredibly informative if you have a thick skin and don't get offended easily. If you do get offended…sorry, not sorry.

Introduction

It was 0300, and I'd been up for about twenty-one hours already. My eyelids were heavy at this point, and I was doing my best to be on point. I'd spent the last two nights drinking with my newfound friends, or shipmates as we call them (most of us used that term in the derogatory sense while I was still in, but it now has a different connotation for me). This was the first time I could drink legally, and dammit if I wasn't going to do everything I could to make the most of it.

The jet lag from my halfway around the world flight to Bahrain from San Francisco hadn't worn off, and the reality of my new situation hadn't yet set in. Freedom was still a luxury I thought I had, and I was told to take advantage of it—so I did.

Now those delicious Hurricanes that I pounded down in that oddly American-style bar in the heart of Muslim country in Bahrain a few hours earlier were stirring like a hurricane in my gut and head!

"Fuck! Don't act like a fucking dumbass drunk!" I kept thinking to myself.

It was my first deployment and the first time I was going to put the past eighteen months of grueling nuclear power training to use. It was time to start the reactor, get the engine room running, and get our asses underway. We were only a few months post-9/11, and our job was to patrol the Persian Gulf for potential threats from Pakistan, Iran, or Iraq.

The guys sitting around me in the "horseshoe," the small U-shaped section in the engine room where several circuit breakers were located, had already been underway for about three months, and they had only had about seventy-two hours of liberty (time off in port) before they had to drag their similarly drunken asses in to start up a billion-dollar engine room to get our submarine underway.

I went to grab the manuals as I was instructed, but in my semi-drunken stupor, I knocked the four-foot-long retaining bar off the shelf, and it landed with an incredibly outrageous *CLANG!*

"Jesus fucking Christ, Barnes!" roared one of my new "buddies," Halsey.[2]

Halsey was a second-class at the time I met him, and he looked like an old cancer survivor: skinny, ghost white, slightly red stubble on his face and head, and cheek bones that looked like they could break a brick wall. We teased him (only after we became friends, of course) that he had "old-man strength." The kind of strength that you can't describe, but you envision your grandfather having when he goes to turn a wrench, slips, cracks his knuckles on the nearby bolt, and you hear the bolt start to whimper while his knuckles start to bleed—yet he never makes a sound. That kind of strength.

Everyone else looked at me through their bloodshot eyes with disgust and frustration.

"Fucking nub!" another murmured under his breath.

I was a nub at that point—a Non-Useful Body.[3] An oxygen drain. A warm body to fill a need. A glorified janitor that the Navy had invested hundreds of thousands of dollars to train.

I collected the books, which weighed as much as the entire Encyclopedia Britannica I read in high school (which by the way, never prepared me for what I was about to experience) and made my way to the horseshoe. The Engineer

---

[2]. I've changed most of the names to protect the innocent. The stupid aren't protected, but the innocent, yes.

[3]. I never have and never will claim to be politically correct. There are plenty of nubs out there in the world today, and for some reason many of them end up as government employees (yes, I get the irony of that statement).

was there, and if I didn't know better, I would have thought he'd had one too many himself.

"No way all of us drunk assholes are going to start up a nuclear reactor!?!" I kept thinking to myself.

"Alright, Petty Officer Barnes, open up the startup procedure and let's begin" the Engineer instructed me.

"Fuck! I can't remember where that is!" I panicked.

After seeing my clueless expression, Roper, a senior mechanic from North Carolina with a chip on his shoulder, demanded, "Give it to me, you fucking nub!" as he grabbed the books from my clumsy hands. He could tell I was lost, and although he did it with the intent of humiliating me, he sure saved me from what could have been the most embarrassing moment of that day.

"Step one…don't let fucking nubs touch anything!" he continued through the dip in his lip with his southern hillbilly accent. The whole group laughed, woke up a little, and we got to work.

A few hours later, after turning valves, energizing equipment, drawing rods, and drinking as much water as we could between evolutions, the reactor was critical (that's a good thing), steam was coming down the headers, turbines were humming along, we were generating electricity, and the boat was ready to get underway.

Being a Navy Nuc (pronounced "Nuke," how sailors in the nuclear power field are referred to) is never a glamorous job. *K-19: The Widow Maker* or *Das Boot* are likely the closest things you can watch that might give you a sense of what happens on a submarine, but even those are filled with lies, exaggerations, and Hollywood bullshit to sell the movies.[4]

What this book is about is how you, as a business owner, can somehow manage to have a bunch of drunken idiots, barely out of school in many cases, able to operate at the highest levels of their potential to get your business humming like a well-oiled machine. If you're still reading this intro, you're in for a treat. Most people have probably already been offended and stopped reading, put the book back on the shelf, or tossed it out.

Doesn't matter to me. I don't give a shit about them.

I give a shit about you. I give a shit about what you are about to learn, and how it's going to make a difference for you, your business, your life, and the world.

I'm on a mission. A mission to change and enhance businesses by grabbing their leaders by the throats[5] and showing them how to turn their great ideas and intentions into great businesses.

I want this book to be a wakeup call to all those business owners, CEOs, entrepreneurs, and executives who continue to follow the herd right off the cliff to obscurity. I see it happen regularly, and it worries me. I worry because I know there is great value in what you do and what you have to offer, but you have been beat down by the media, by politicians, by bureaucrats and regulators,[6] and some even by your families and employees.

You're operating your business in a way that is sure to guarantee failure. Maybe not today or even in the next five years, but someday.

But who am I to give you advice on your business? What could I add to the conversation you haven't heard elsewhere? My take, though not politically

---

4. Fucking Hollywood. Dramatize everything and make you think it's cooler than it really is. They can sell a screenplay, but if they ever had to spend a night on an actual sub, I bet they'd fire their million-dollar agents the next day and have PTSD for years to come.
5. Because I can't grab them by the balls…some of the best leaders don't have them. ☺
6. Fucking government.

correct by any stretch, is to help you understand how the principles that continue to help the U.S. Navy maintain an unblemished record of nuclear power operation and the highest military standards of all time, all while operating in intense situations hundreds of feet below the ocean surface, can help you develop systems, processes, and procedures to help you grow your revenue and profits.

I have been a submariner, a blue-collar mechanic performing some of the nastiest jobs ever (which you'll get to hear more about in these pages), and a director of a Global Fortune 100 company. I've been tasked with helping startups get off the ground, helping employees become intrapreneurs, and coaching teams on innovation and product development, and I've managed a remote team of twenty-five people across the western United States.

Additionally, I've run projects spanning the globe to help an already successful company grow its market share and dominate in this new technologically driven era—a challenge not easily overcome for a 150-year-old company with deep roots in traditional operations. I've helped develop a startup culture in an old company, been a driving force for innovation and change, and trained hundreds of people across the world on how to use technology and innovative thinking to grow their businesses.

In this book, I am going to attempt to relate my education, my experiences, and my insights into how to run a business properly so you can not only survive but thrive and lead the field in your industry.

If you're an entrepreneur, CEO, or executive of a large business, this will help you immensely. However, if you're an entitled little shit who thinks you should be given the keys to the kingdom without first putting in the work, then read on and learn what it takes to take charge.

This book is about becoming the captain of your ship by using the tried and true principles of the U.S. Nuclear Navy Submarine force to turn your ship around and get all hands rowing in the right direction.

It's about taking control of your destiny and becoming the leader you must be to succeed.

It's about Getting All Hands on Deck.

Background

First, you reading this book means more to me than I can convey. If you have made it through the introduction, and hopefully had a little chuckle, then I think you'll enjoy what is written on the pages ahead.

Regardless of whether you continue reading or not, I want to convey my gratitude.

Thank you.

This book came about because I was specifically told by mentors that I ought to write something about how my Naval experience translates into the business world. Perhaps it will help you.

I was never an officer, let alone the captain, of a ship in the Navy, but I have been the captain of my own ship for a while now. Having started a few businesses myself (some massive failures, others successes), I can appreciate the hard work and effort you deal with daily.

My life wasn't illustrious prior to joining the Navy. It wasn't hard, but it wasn't all sunshine and roses. Our family left California in 1994 after gangs, bad business, and the Northridge earthquake shook my parents to the core. We lived in a travel trailer, a motel, and with friends before everything stabilized again and we could move back into a real house.

Throughout that entire time, my dad, my idol, never gave up and never gave in to the circumstances. Regardless of how bad and bleak it may have seemed to them, my brother, sister, and I always had food in our bellies and a shelter over our heads. I will never forget my dad's relentless persistence in providing for us.

It is likely his dedication to us, his own business, and his friends that made me who I am today. It is because of my dad that I am here writing this book for you.

An Oath

Every service member, enlisted or officer, every politician, or anyone who has taken a position that could somehow affect the security of our country is required to take an oath. I still remember the day I took that oath in Denver prior to being shipped to Great Lakes National Training Center (boot camp) on July 5, 2000.

Just twenty-four hours earlier, I was enjoying a beer with my buddies Jesse, Rob, and Taylor at Rob's house while watching some fireworks. We had graduated high school a couple of months earlier, and I had no clue what I wanted to do in life but was already sworn to the Navy. I ruined my shoulder during my sophomore year by playing baseball in Australia, and my other buddy made sure it never healed when he dislocated it that fall at football practice. If it weren't for that, I probably would have gone to college to play baseball—my only true love in life at that point.

In all honesty, that ruined shoulder is ultimately what led me to my oath, and eventually here, writing this book for you. I think it was the universe's way of telling me that there was so much more for me to do and experience, and even become, than being an athlete. So, John, if you're reading this, thanks for being the best damn high school running back I've ever seen and for making sure I followed the path I was meant to follow!

Now, the oath:

> *I, Jeff Barnes, do solemnly swear that I will support and defend the Constitution of the United States of America, from all enemies, foreign and domestic;*
>
> *that I will bear true faith and allegiance to the same;*
>
> *and that I will obey the orders of the President of the United States and the orders of the officers appointed over me, according to regulations and the Uniform Code of Military Justice.*
>
> *So help me God.*

This oath is sacred to me for reasons that can only be understood by having lived and breathed it every day of my life for several years.

I believe that an oath or affirmation like this is an important part of defining who a person is. I am sad to see that in many parts of our country, we don't have oaths like this for our children anymore.

However, I am happy to see that in many institutions where the government hasn't asserted its will, we are seeing patriotism alive and free. I still remember the Pledge of Allegiance being said every day before school started, and I believe that repetition and reminder of where we live, how we got here, and who made those sacrifices for us to be here is vitally important to the continued prosperity of our country.

If you haven't said the Pledge of Allegiance lately, I encourage you to read this and be reminded of what it is that allows you to do what you enjoy and be who you are:

> *I pledge allegiance to the flag*
>
> *Of the United States of America,*
>
> *And to the Republic for which it stands,*
>
> *One nation, under God, indivisible,*
>
> *With liberty and justice for all!*

Now I am not a very religious person, but I do believe that our removing this from our schools and communities has been a part of what divides our country to this day. If you don't believe in God or if you call Him something else, so be it. But remember that it is our Constitution and flag that give you the liberties and freedoms that allow you build the business and life you desire.

And please, take a moment to silently thank all those men and women who have given their lives to make this possible for you and me.

Before I get started, I want to let you know there will be several new terms introduced throughout this book that I will attempt to explain in parentheses as you come across them. At the end of the book, I have a glossary of terms that could be either hilarious, helpful, or disturbing depending on your disposition. If you're easily offended, maybe don't read on…just a thought.

Now, let's get your business running like a well-oiled machine!

Chapter One
The Best Laid Plans

"All ahead Flank, Cavitate!" was the order called up by the captain from the bridge. The responding bell was called up right away in the control room, acknowledging the order.

"Right full rudder!"

Captain O'Kane was barking orders down the hatch from the bridge on the topside of the submarine, sweat dripping from his brow even though they were under the cover of darkness off the coast of Taiwan. The crew was amped up, every hair standing on end, and the tension was palpable. The last several weeks had been a blur for the men tasked with helping secure a U.S. victory in the Pacific during World War II.

The U.S. was maneuvering to end the war in the Pacific, push the Japanese back, and disable their fleet. The crew of the USS Tang (SS-306) was using every ounce of its energy to accomplish this mission.

The captain had spotted enemy freighters carrying planes, cargo, and troops traveling in a convoy along the coast of China in the Formosa Straight and was determined to take out the convoy. The Tang carried twenty-four torpedoes aboard the boat and wouldn't return to port with any unused armament in its tubes.

The crew was on the tail end of a thirty-day mission to intercept enemy ships in the Formosa Straight, where they had sunk seven enemy ships in the past two weeks. During that battle, late in the evening of October 24, 1944, Commander O'Kane pulled the boat back to load the last two torpedoes into the forward tubes in preparation to return and sink the last remaining transport ship before heading back to port.

Rations were running low and the diesel fuel was becoming a concern when the Tang fired its last torpedo at the enemy transport ship. The crew was exuberant and ready to turn tail back to its safe haven, knowing that it had just sent the last of its offense out of the tubes to chalk up yet another notch on the proverbial belt.

> *But it wasn't time to celebrate yet...*

This book is about how you can begin to integrate principles into your life and business pulled from the rich history and culture of the U.S. Navy's submarine force. Submariner culture dates to the USS Holland (SS-1), which was commissioned in 1900.

Being a submariner means honoring a code that has been around for more than a century; it is one of the few brotherhoods remaining where that code is understood even if it is never spoken.

The submariner's code ensures that, no matter the circumstance, he will do what is necessary to ensure the safety and survival of his fellow crewmembers and complete the mission. Submariners have a different language that is hardly understood even by others of the Navy, let alone civilians on the outside looking in.

They move and act a little differently—with focused determination and steadfast resolve to complete the mission. This mentality is born from stories of the heritage of submarine life, handed down from one salty sailor to another.

The sea stories become legends that illustrate to each sailor what it means to be a submariner. They demonstrate the guiding principles and core values to which one must adhere to survive a life in a black steel tube hundreds of feet below the surface.

The training submariners undergo is designed to prevent and mitigate catastrophes wherever possible and ensure the success of the missions.

However, even considering all the training and hard work each sailor puts in, there is still the chance that things will go wrong. That is why this book will outline the strategies you can use to mitigate challenges in your life and business, and more importantly, guide you on how to develop the mental toughness to bounce back in the face of adversity.

It will also help you, as the leader of yourself and others, to develop the mindset and skills you need to make the difficult choices when the time comes. Being submarine-tough doesn't mean you win every battle, but it does mean that if for whatever reason you do fail, you will find the strength to carry on smartly.

At 0230 (spoken "zero two-thirty" or "oh two-thirty") on October 25, 1944, the USS Tang (SS-306) prepared to fire its last two remaining torpedoes at the last remaining transport ship.

"Torpedoes ready, sir," came the call from below decks.

"Set...fire!" the order blasted from the bridge.

The first torpedo let loose straight and true in the water, bound straight for the transport. The second torpedo surfaced and began acting erratically. The watch on the bridge and the captain both knew this meant trouble. Torpedoes are meant to course-correct along their path and use a magnetic trigger to activate and detonate the warhead. Unfortunately, the torpedo lacked a safety shutoff device in the event it headed in the wrong direction.

The Mark-18 torpedo made a U-turn, sensing the Tang's magnetic field, and headed straight for the boat. It was at this point that Commander O'Kane ordered the ship to move full speed ahead, conducting fishtail maneuvers to avoid the collision. The torpedo could travel at speeds upwards of twenty-nine knots, far faster than the Tang could ring up a bell and distance itself from the impending danger.

The General Alarm was sounded with all hands being ordered to "brace for impact!"

It was no use. The torpedo was too fast and collided with the aft end of the submarine, causing a massive explosion that left a hole in the hull of the ship. Although the boat surfaced, the seawater poured in uncontrollably and immediately sank the aft end.

The bow of the ship remained nose-up with its ballast tanks still full of air.

In the midst of the chaos, with the lives of his crew in his hands and the boat certain to sink in a wartime disaster, Commander O'Kane ordered his crew to "Close the hatch!"

At that point, the bridge hatch was shut to prevent the ship from flooding through the control room, with O'Kane and two other men remaining topside, certain that they would be washed away. The order was given in a desperate attempt to save the boat from sinking and to give the men below a fighting chance to evacuate the sinking vessel.

Men below forced the control room door shut along with the lower hatch in the conning tower, and in a matter of seconds, water stopped flowing in from the forward compartment.

The men remaining topside on the bridge were washed to sea, including O'Kane. Seeking an opportunity to take out one of the deadliest submarines of the Pacific battle, Japanese escort ships launched a series of depth charges near the submarine, delaying and preventing escape efforts from the crew still on board the boat. The battery compartment flooded and caught fire, releasing a cloud of chlorine gas that could erupt into flames at any moment.

The remaining crewmen below attempted to make their way to the forward torpedo room and escape the wreckage through the forward escape hatch. Of the forty remaining crewmen who made their way to the hatch, only thirteen made it out before the ship was either fully flooded or the crew suffocated from lack of oxygen and a burning battery compartment.

Of the eighty-seven crewmen on board, seventy-eight perished after the ship came to rest in 180 feet of seawater near the coast of China. Nine crewmen survived the ordeal, including Commander O'Kane, who were found in the sea the next morning by a Japanese patrol boat.

The survivors were imprisoned for the remainder of the war, suffering beatings, starvation, hypothermia, and many other maladies we would find hard to fathom today. When O'Kane was released from prison in August 1945 after the peace treaty was signed, he weighed a measly eighty-eight pounds. He went on to become a Rear Admiral of the U.S. Navy and earned the Medal of Honor (Adams 2017).

Commander O'Kane and his crew conducted five patrols during the short two years their boat was active. During that time, they sank thirty-one enemy war ships, rescued twenty-two airmen who were shot down in battle. The Tang's run is now considered to have been "one of the greatest submarine cruises of all time"[7] (Adams 2017).

During the Second World War, the U.S. submarine service accounted for only 1.6 percent of the U.S. Navy but accounted for 55 percent of the Japanese maritime losses. Over 1,300 enemy ships were sunk, over 16,000 enemies killed, and over 53,000 wounded because of submarine warfare.

To say that the submarine service was effective and responsible for the progress the U.S. Navy made during the Second World War would be an understatement. The Japanese and German militaries spared no expense in

---

[7]. These were badass sailors. These are the types of men who helped coin the phrase "crusty old sailor" because they lived and died at sea, never giving a second thought to the sacrifice they were making.

figuring out how to disable, dismantle, and destroy U.S. submarines to further their efforts in the Second World War.

Owing to the success of the submarine force in WWII and the ability of these vessels to carry out missions without being detected, the U.S. Navy sought ways to improve on the design and operation of the diesel submarines of the day, and thus was born the nuclear power era of submarine propulsion.

On September 30, 1954, the USS Nautilus (SSN-571) was commissioned under the command of Cmdr. Eugene Wilkinson. The USS Nautilus was the first nuclear-powered submarine in the U.S. Navy fleet and went on to mark the beginning of an era that has since changed the landscape of maritime war, reconnaissance, and our understanding of nuclear theory.

The dog-fighting days of World War II and Commander O'Kane's USS *Tang* may be far behind us now, but the systems, processes, procedures, and technology that came out of the U.S. Navy's "Silent Service" have endured and created one of the longest lasting track records of success the world has ever known.

Whereas commercial nuclear power plants like that of Chernobyl and Three-Mile Island create fear and doubt around nuclear power, the U.S. Navy has an unblemished record of operation of nuclear power plants for over sixty years! This is owing to the extreme discipline of the crewmembers who man these vessels, as well as the unending training, qualification, systems, processes, and procedures that are developed to ensure safe and successful operation.

I will attempt in this book to outline how you too can begin to implement similar systems, processes, and procedures that will ensure the long-term success of your enterprise, even if you aren't required to navigate the globe undersea with no more than a compass and a map! The day-to-day operations of running a small single-location private practice, a Global Fortune 100 company, or a nuclear-powered submarine may differ dramatically in appearance, but in premise they all center around one common theme: the successful completion of a mission.

The fact is that there are certain ways to get things done, and it doesn't matter if you are loading a torpedo tube, preparing to fire on an enemy combatant, or running a mid-sized financial services company; if there is a goal that needs to be achieved, you must take the right steps, in the right order, with the right people, with the right focus to make it all happen.

The USS Tang was not considered one of the greatest submarines of WWII by accident. Commander O'Kane had been on multiple ships prior to his command of the *Tang*, and during that time he learned several core characteristics that lend themselves to the successful completion of a mission.

The next several chapters of this book are going to outline the key components to running your business successfully, prepare you for the ever-changing world of technology and communication, and show you how you can begin to apply militaristic processes to your organization to help you run everything like you are the captain of your ship. You will get to read some humorous accounts of my time in the Navy and apply the lessons I have learned from both the military and my time with a Fortune 100 company to your business for continued and sustained growth. If you apply these lessons and begin to implement the systems, processes, procedures, and traits I outline in this book, you will be light-years ahead of your competition and ready to navigate any stormy sea that finds its way to your front door.

What has made submarines so successful over the past century is a combination of grit and principles. Submariners like those on the Tang are a not uncommon in the submarine community. In this widely unknown and misunderstood world you will find a culture that thrives in the face of adversity and prides itself on time honored traditions and principles that are reinforced through diligent training and sound systems.

Structuring your business in such a way that it is immune to failure is impossible. However, developing the right systems and fortifying them with your convictions and principles will help you to recover from any failure with minimal damage.

Although the story of the USS Tang does not end happily ever after, it does illustrate how a well-run organization with top-notch training and systems in place can accomplish incredible feats. If it weren't for a faulty torpedo, we would be telling a different story today.

Most of us will never be faced with a life-and-death situation such as Commander O'Kane was on that fateful day. However, as a leader you will be faced with challenging situations that training alone won't prepare you for. It is for that reason you must develop principles, structures, and systems to guide and help you when your training falls short. This book aims to help you make that happen.

Chapter Two
Captain You?

It's widely accepted that if you are going to lead men and women into battle, you must first gain their trust and admiration. History is littered with accounts of battles lost and won due to the bravery of the men who fought. In almost every story you read of a "David vs. Goliath" situation, you can typically find an account of the man leading the charge being the sole reason for the victory.

Why is that?

We know full well that one person cannot defeat an entire army of better-armed opponents, yet we see that time and again it is one person who is given the credit for a victory. It is the captain of the ship who receives the Presidential Unit Citation on behalf of his crew, for a very good reason.

The captain of the ship is the person who is ultimately responsible for the crew and contents. It doesn't matter what goes wrong: the captain is ultimately to blame. This also means that when things go right, the captain receives the commendation and praise.

The *Wall Street Journal* doesn't honor the code developer who creates the software that powers the latest internet technology—it honors the CEO who makes sure it sees the light of day and creates the impact it deserves.

The MVP of the Super Bowl is almost always the quarterback—the captain of the team leading them to victory.

The man or woman who *commands*[8] the most respect in a military unit is the highest ranking officer. Many times this person is also deserving of that respect as they have earned it over the course of their careers and have learned how to manage teams and people for maximum effectiveness.

Moreover, they have learned how to instill certain qualities in the people who work for them to allow the unit to prosper. They have spent time working on their leadership skills and abilities, communicate a strong and clear vision to their team, and ultimately hold people accountable for results.

These characteristics are the mark of a true *Commander CEO*®, a person who exhibits the leadership qualities that earn him the respect of the people who work for him and, in so doing, can command the results that are needed to ensure mission success.

The fact is that you are, as the captain of your own ship, ultimately responsible for the outcome of your business. Whether it lives, dies, or simply bobs on the water is all up to you. Your job as the commander of your company is to instill the right qualities in your team that will lead to the success you desire or need to defeat your competition.

Now here's the funny thing—in business, there is rarely competition externally. Sure, we see GM and Ford going at it daily, or Verizon beating up on Sprint and vice versa, but that is simply because they are fighting over the same slice of pie. In all reality, most businesses do not have such competition because they can simply go after another pie altogether.

In the end, the only true competition is between yourself and your ability to lead. It is the leader who can ultimately cobble together nearly any resources he needs to turn a great idea into a great business. Napoleon Hill, in one of his many lectures on how to create breakthrough success, said:

---

8. If you don't "command" respect and people don't look up to you, the worst thing you can do is "demand" respect. Nothing will help you lose the respect of your followers faster than asserting yourself as the authority. Demonstrate, don't demand.

> It would seem impossible for a man to succeed in any undertaking unless he was formally educated in that field. Thomas Edison was perhaps the greatest inventor the world had ever known. He was dealing all the time with science, yet he knew nothing at all about science. Andrew Carnegie told me that he personally didn't know anything about the making or even the marketing of steel. He said he could always surround himself with men who knew those things, and that he was most valuable for what he did not know: what couldn't be done; why it had to take so long. (Hill 1937)

What Hill was discussing here was Edison and Carnegies' ability to lead others in the pursuit of a vision. We know the names in history not because they *did* something incredible, but most likely because they led others in creating something incredible!

Henry Ford did not create the V-8 engine or the assembly line. Instead, he surrounded himself with the right people, gave them a vision to work toward, made it happen, and then got all the credit.[9]

You see, the important thing is to not be the one *doing* everything that you think is important. It is more important to spend your time cultivating your abilities to lead others and then finding a way to rally them to a cause.

How do you do this? If you aren't a great orator or visionary, is it possible to instill people with a sense of purpose and pride that will sufficiently motivate them to your cause?

Of course it is! But it all begins with the right vision!

---

9. Side note—he also demanded they figure out what was considered impossible at the time, and as a result an entire industry of powerful cars and trucks was transformed. If you don't demand results, you won't get any. We talk about this later.

Chapter Three
Damn the Torpedoes!

"Damn the torpedoes! Full speed ahead!"

Admiral David Farragut's orders were passed from ship to ship to move forward in the Battle of Mobile Bay during the Civil War. The Confederate fleet had devised underwater mines, known then as torpedoes, to protect the bay and prevent the Federal fleet from advancing into the bay. When Farragut saw his ships slowing and retreating, he ordered them into action to push past the mines and overtake the bay.

The capture of Mobile Bay was paramount to the Union's success in the Gulf of Mexico. The Union knew that to win the battle in the South, they needed to blockade the Confederate forces from the Gulf and shut down their supply lines. Doing so would further defeat and demoralize the remaining Confederate troops.

The Battle of Mobile Bay was also important when you consider that it was the last stand of the Confederacy's naval forces. To keep the bay secure, the Confederates had rigged the bay with explosives to avert the Union Navy and hold them at sea long enough for the long-range cannons of the forts to take a toll.

When Farragut ordered the ships to move ahead, they complied, and rather easily took the bay and eventually forced the surrender of the final Confederate ship, the CSS *Tennessee*. This victory for the Union helped bring the Civil War to a close just a few months later.[10]

When you consider the directives that you are giving your team and your organization, how clear are they?

How clear are your people on why they are doing what they're doing in the first place?

Are people simply going through the motions to collect a paycheck, or are they committed to a process that is part of something bigger than they are?

A vision is something that transcends our own individual abilities, instills a sense of pride and hope, and ultimately helps us define who we are as people. A great vision allows you to bring the right people to your cause and keep them longer than a half-hearted vision does.

A vision gives you a shining light to keep moving toward in hopes you will eventually find that rainbow.

Most companies pay lip service to their vision because they don't understand the profound importance it plays in everything they do. At your company, a lack of vision results in a lack of direction or focus and can lead to an untimely demise.

A great vision, however, transcends time and generations and continues to build upon itself.

This isn't a book about creating a vision, but it is a book about making you the captain of your ship and getting your business on the right track.

---

10. This may seem an oversimplification, but the story goes down as legend. Why? Because it was the determination of the leader and his men to see the vision through to completion. Without those two components—vision and leadership—no organization will prosper for long.

If you fail to have a vision for your company, how can you expect people working for you to have any pride in what they do?

You can't, because they won't know where their leader is taking them. Sorry to say it, but as the person in charge, the boss, the CEO, the founder, the entrepreneur—whatever you are in your business—if you haven't spent time cultivating a great vision that you can stand behind, put up on the side of a building, and shout from the rooftops (or the depths of the sea), then you don't have something that will rally people.

If you can't rally people to what you want to achieve, then everything else I'm going to tell you in this book is of no use.

A submarine captain knows all the inner workings of his ship, and has the utmost respect for his crew because he knows what it takes to get such a massive vessel underway and sailing smoothly. He also knows that each person understands they are part of something bigger than themselves—bigger than their boat and even bigger than their mission—and in almost every case they are willing to take their last breath to uphold that vision.

The U.S. Navy's vision is to bring security, democracy, peace, and prosperity to the American people and to protect America's citizens, interests, and friends anytime and anywhere they may be at risk.

This vision is what inspires approximately 40,000 people to enlist or join the Navy every year, and similar visions for other military branches enlist an additional 140,000 people every single year. How does your vision stack up?

Many people still get confused by vision and mission statements, so let me try to clear it up here if I can.

First, the vision is the long-term horizon—what you want the world to look like some day. Many times it doesn't have an end date or a number when you can say it has been achieved.

A mission is something that helps you achieve that vision.

The Navy's mission is "…To maintain, train and equip combat-ready Naval forces capable of winning wars, deterring aggression and maintaining freedom of the seas."

You can see that the thing they are *doing* is a mission, and the thing they hope to *achieve* is a vision. They are *maintaining, training, and equipping*—doing actions.

Another way to look at this is by putting all of it into a simple diagram that helps illustrate the point. As you can see here, the vision is the overarching theme to your company, with the mission being something we want to do to achieve that vision. We can change missions as we see fit—maybe you've achieved one mission and want to start on the next, or maybe the environment has changed and you are adapting to that change. Either way, you can change out the mission, and thereby the strategies, systems, tools, and technologies that help you achieve that mission.

However, your *vision* should remain unchanged because it is something you and your company stand for and believe in, and hopefully that will not change.

The vision drives the mission, which in turn helps to define the strategy. From there, we look at what systems would help in executing that strategy. The strategy requires certain tactics to be used, and those tactics rely on different types of technology, which can be implemented with certain tools.

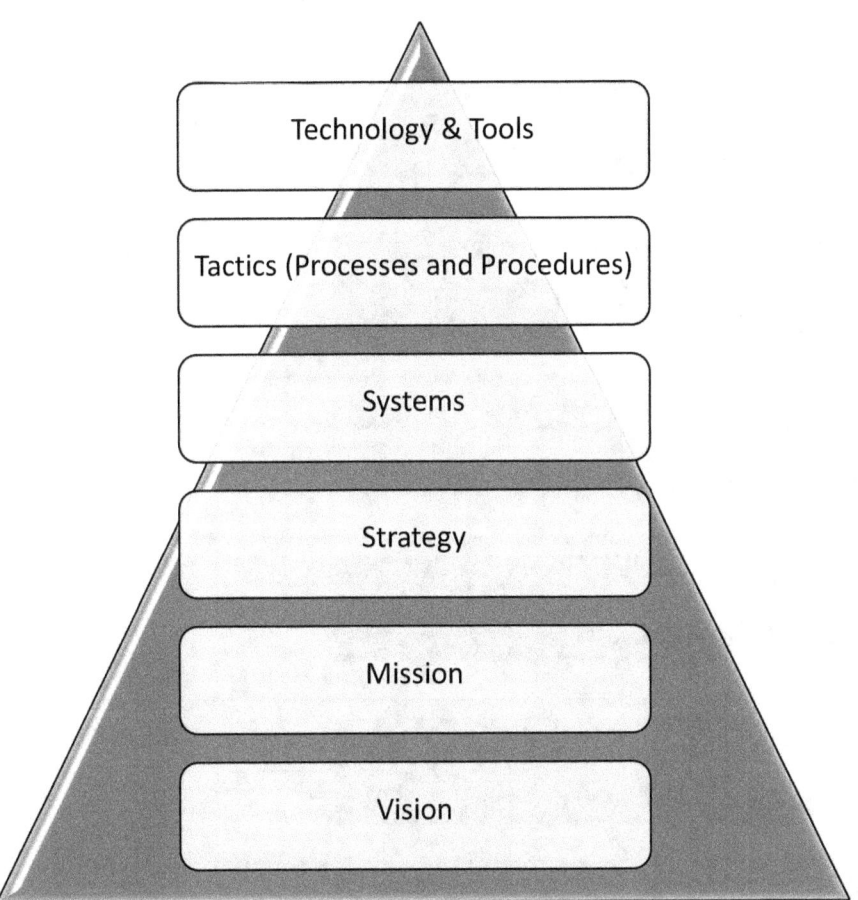

Here is an example of how the vision impacts what you and your team do on a daily and weekly basis:

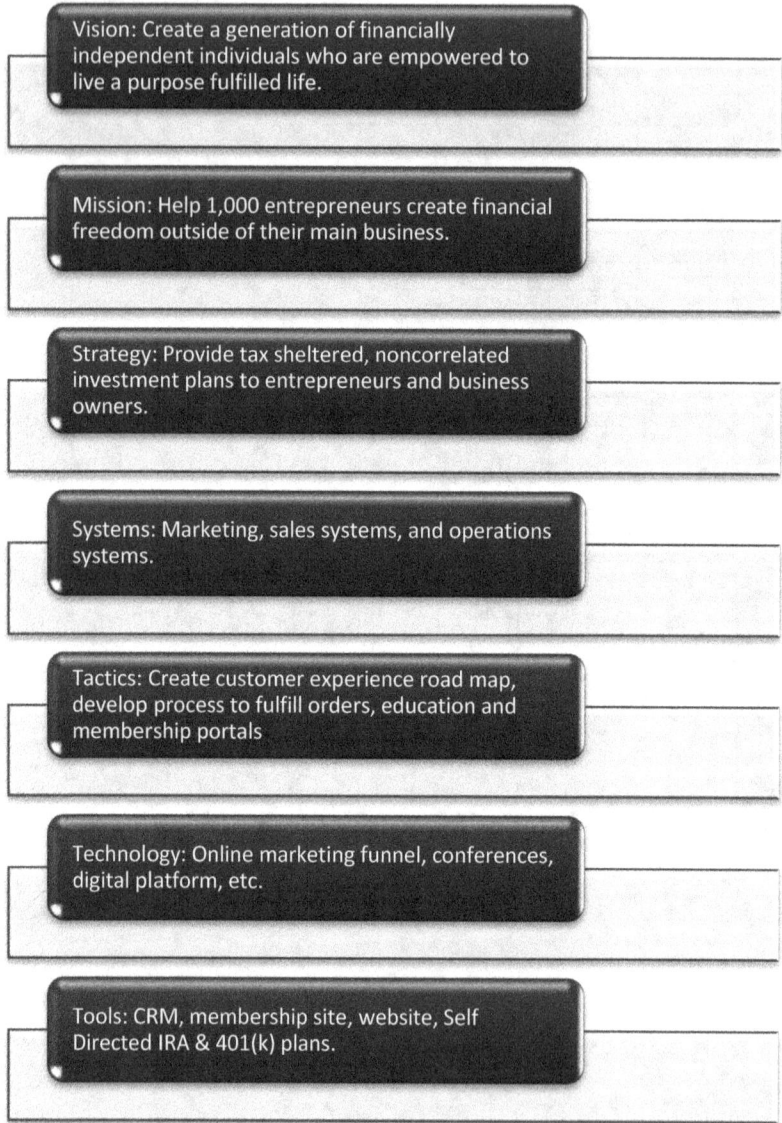

Here's the funny thing to note: the "thing" we were selling was the bottom of the entire setup. Most businesses go about this all wrong—they start with their "thing" and then try to find a way to fit that into the market. If you instead start with your vision of what you want to achieve in the world or your business, then work down from there, you will find the right "thing" by working through these processes.

Another challenge that most entrepreneurs and CEOs face is that they don't have a personal vision for their lives, and therefore the vision for their business, or what they do in their business, feels incongruent with who they see themselves as. For example, my first shot at business was in 2003 while I was still in the Navy.

My buddy Nick came to this "Opportunity" meeting with me to learn how to become financially independent at a time when we were both spending our money on liquor and girls. Or rather, spending our money on liquor in hopes we could figure out a way to get the girls.

My mom turned me onto this company and I obliged her and went to the meeting. The speaker was so compelling that both Nick and I signed up for this program. See if you can spot the irony here…

The opportunity meeting that we went to sold us on the idea of becoming financial planners for people who were in the same situation that we were in, which, to say the least, was without money or without a financial plan!

We signed up and were completely gung ho about the opportunity to help other people with their finances as we learned to do the exact same thing for ourselves. Looking back on it, I can only shrug and shake my head at what a terrible idea it was for me to embark on this mission to begin with. I learned a great deal about finance, so I'm not upset about that, but ask me how many customers I obtained in the several years that I actually "worked" for this organization…

Zero!

Now, I helped many people with their financial plans, and went over financial planning and understanding finances, but I **GOT ABSOLUTELY NO CUSTOMERS!**[11]

What I have since learned is that my vision for myself was completely out of line with becoming a financial planner. I had almost no desire to talk to people about setting up a financial plan, buying life insurance, or investing in mutual funds. I didn't see myself as a salesperson (back then, at least), and was completely unconfident about my ability to talk to people about finances. This one reason alone should have been enough for me to stay clear of this organization and say no to the opportunity. However, the person who was selling me into the opportunity was absolutely clear on their vision, and it was in complete alignment with what they were trying to do. They had the power in the situation, and thus I onboarded into a company that I didn't fully believe in—and the results spoke for themselves.

Nick was a little bit smarter than me. He quit within a few months whereas I stuck around for a few years.

So you see, the importance of having a vision for yourself and aligning that vision to your business, and then taking that vision and turning it into a mission and a strategy is vitally important to the success of any organization. When you fail to have a vision for what you want to achieve, you end up chasing down any potential tactic, tool, or technology in the hopes that you will someday achieve a goal, but if that goal is not to ensure alignment with your vision for your company, it will be very tough to stay focused and motivated to achieve that goal, and in turn, it will be twice as hard to motivate the people who work for you.

When Adm. Farragut forced his fleet to advance through a naval minefield that could have easily sunk his ships and killed the entire crew on board, he didn't

---

11. It really sucks to give all of your time and energy and not get compensated for it. You feel like an idiot for longer than you care to imagine and begin to doubt your entire purpose. The solution is to implement the systems that will attract customers to you who are ready, willing, and able to spend money with you. More on that later in the book.

do it because he was wishy-washy about his goal. He did it because he had a conviction that he thoroughly believed in, all stemming from a vision for a unified country. If it wasn't for that vision that he and others shared of having a unified country, it would've been very difficult for him to command his crew into a mission that could likely end their lives.

You may think that your business is different and that you don't need a vision or mission statement to help motivate your team to do a job. That may be true to an extent, but unfortunately it makes it twice as hard to be the true leader of your business and the manager that you want to be. It prevents you from having a clear communication plan that allows people to understand what it is that you want to achieve, and thus people are less willing and able to follow orders because they don't understand what the outcome needs to be.

Even though we had no idea what the actual mission was while working in the engine room on our submarine, we knew what the vision and our purpose was on that boat: to protect and defend the Constitution of the United States against all enemies! We knew, or rather we trusted, that the leaders at the helm were doing their part to uphold that same ideal, and therefore we fell in line and did our jobs.

If you want your team, your employees, and even your customers to do the same for you, then it is imperative that you begin with a vision that transcends your business and yourself. Only after that can you begin to lead as if you are really the captain of your ship!

Chapter Four
Leading with Systems

"Motherfucker! You have to be fucking kidding me!"

We had already been on shift for more than eight hours, with very little sleep the last two nights due to this impending operation, and now, with the reactor up and running and the loops getting warm, we found out that somebody had really fucked up![12]

We were sitting pierside at Puget Sound Naval Shipyard in Bremerton, Washington, and we were doing what was called a "fast cruise." Essentially, our ship had just undergone eighteen months of upgrading, modernizing, and extensive maintenance conducted by both crew and shipyard personnel. To say that we were ready to get the hell out of Dodge was an understatement. Here we were, a young crew of twenty-something men being transported from their home port of San Diego, California up to Washington to live in a big black tube for over a year with very little view of sunlight, never mind the bikini-clad bodies we left behind, and we were ready to get going.

For the past several months, many of us had spent twelve to eighteen out of every twenty-four hours in the shipyard, working on equipment, fixing systems, and spending countless hours on administrative paperwork, not to mention going behind the shipyard and fixing things that they hadn't done correctly, and we were, quite simply, over it! This fast cruise was a test of all our systems to ensure that we could get the boat back underway and out of Bremerton. We were all looking forward to finally letting the sun set in the Pacific Northwest and heading down to sunny San Diego once again.

---

12. Not uncommon in any major organization or division, but how you respond determines whether it is a catastrophe or just a learning opportunity.

Unfortunately, as we were opening valves one by one to bring steam down the header, we noticed that one steam trap, a device meant to keep condensation from damaging equipment downstream, was installed backwards. This type of oversight had been happening regularly as crew and shipyard personnel clashed over the right way and wrong way to do things, and those of us who were about to live on the boat were ready to just get things fixed. Every time this happened it resulted in several days' delay, mountains of paperwork, and more finger-pointing than you would find at a mime convention!

Luckily for us, it was about 2300 (i.e. 11 PM), which meant that many the crew were already in their racks and many of the senior management personnel were just as tired and frustrated as we were that things weren't moving. When I proposed that we simply isolate the steam trap with a header still hot and replace the trap without shutting down our systems, I expected to hear a barrage of derogatory comments come my way.

To my surprise, everyone was on board with this quick, efficient, and safe repair. Lucky for me, or rather, I think for everyone else, I was the quality assurance inspector who was also responsible for writing all the work packages for a large majority of the maintenance we did on this system. I knew the system like the back of my hand and knew we could perform the repair without any issues.

It may seem ludicrous, but this type of process normally takes hours and hours of planning and preparation, and is an administrative nightmare for those of us who don't like admin. When we had the top brass sign off on this idea, my team and I got to work quickly and expeditiously to put the paperwork in place, get the necessary signatures, and begin the work. Within sixty minutes, we were able to finish the work, clear all the tags (meaning clear the safety mechanisms in place), and get the system back up and running.

It was an uncelebrated victory, but a victory nonetheless. We managed to maintain steam in the headers without shutting down the reactor and had an opportunity to stay on schedule. I'm not sure how much it costs to keep a ship in the shipyard every single day, but I know it sure as hell isn't cheap, which is likely why everyone was so willing to allow us to move this along quickly.

However, the other thing that allowed us to move everything along so quickly and easily was that we had systems in place for when we encountered such a situation. We had personnel that were well-trained in what needed to be done, and we had administrative processes and procedures that allowed us to move forward quickly with all the necessary items covered. In this situation, we likely saved the Navy, and thus the taxpayers, $100,000 easily. Granted, if someone was doing their job right to begin with this wouldn't have been an issue, but sometimes things happen that are out of your hands, as discussed earlier, and we simply need to pick up and move on.

This book is about optimizing, innovating, and transforming your business,[13] and to do that you must be willing to look at your business as a series of systems to help you achieve your goals. I learned a long time ago and still live by this motto to this day that you lead people, and you manage systems. However, what I find most people doing is trying to manage people without any systems, processes, or procedures, and as a result they wonder why their business stagnates on a regular basis. Many entrepreneurs and CEOs continue to swim upstream against the river whenever they are trying to grow their business because they haven't quite figured out how to optimize their processes to begin with.

In fact, most businesses don't even have systems in place to do the simplest of things. In the next chapter, I will outline the key systems you must have in order to get your business running smoothly, but before I begin I need you to understand the importance of actually having a system in place.

When I say "system," I don't mean an automatic, technology-driven machine that does things for you. A system, by my definition, is a series of processes, procedures, tools, technology, and people all working harmoniously together to achieve one common objective. Having a system in place allows you to

---

13. More toward the end of the book on that exact process.

pinpoint exactly what the bottlenecks are that prevent you from growing and thus make it hard to actually lead your company in the direction you want it to go.

Imagine, for example, a Viking ship. In these old sloops, men sat next to each other side by side, oars in hand, rowing and pulling in unison to get the ship moving forward in the right direction. Now imagine one column of men rowing in one direction and the other rowing in the opposite direction. The result would be a ship constantly spinning around in a circle on one axis but never going anywhere. The same is true in your business. If you don't have everyone rowing in the same direction, at the same speed, and in unison, then you are likely only succeeding by sheer force of will. This is a recipe for disaster and is ultimately what leads CEOs and business owners to an early grave or at least early retirement.

As before, I want you to understand that there are these things called standard operating procedures, which are part of a giant system to help you and your business run in the right direction. SOPs, as they are commonly referred to in the engineering world, are designed to achieve this goal—get everyone on the same page, moving in the right direction, with the same goal and objective in mind.

Your goal as the leader of your business is to instill this mentality in your team and then have them work in unison with each other. You achieve this by creating standard operating procedures that are laden with systems that allow you to manage the systems rather than manage the people. Once you achieve this, then you can start installing and using technology to manage your business, and you can step back and actually be the leader that you want to be. However, if you continue to *manage* people and try to force them to do things the way you want them to without any rhyme or reason, without any vision or structure, and without any real guidance on what needs to be done consistently on a daily basis to achieve an objective, then you are simply setting yourself up for failure.

When I talk about leading with systems, what I mean is that you are actually managing systems rather than people. You get to spend your time looking at dashboards that give you a clear picture of the business, and this frees up your time to actually go out and work with your employees and use one of the best leadership tactics I can think of: the MBWA (Management By Walking Around). When you have systems up and running, you don't need to spend all of your time barking orders and telling people how to do things. Instead, you get a chance to be the leader, show them the future, and help guide them down that path. This allows your people to do the heavy lifting because now they know what to do, and they have a structure and guidelines on how to get their job done.

Before you begin trying to draft your own standard operating procedures or employee guidelines, let's first look at the five systems you must have in place to actually grow your business.

Chapter Five
Critical Operations

"The reactor is critical![14] Engineering watch supervisor, start up the engine room" blared across the 2MC loudspeaker system in the engine room. Time to get the ship moving.

As a nuc, you're generally required to arrive at the ship several hours before everyone else when preparing to get underway. When the reactor is shut down, it can take several hours to get it back up to the right temperature in order to bring steam down the header. Nuclear fission doesn't occur very well at low temperatures, and low temperatures aren't conducive to creating steam. As a result, we need to spend a significant amount of time starting up the reactor, which increases the temperature of the water inside the reactor thus allowing us to create steam in the secondary loop.

It is this high pressure, high temperature, superheated steam that allows nuclear power plants in both naval ships and commercial applications to operate turbines and other critical machinery that provide propulsion and electricity. It's not like your electric steam kettle sitting on the counter where you can flip a switch and a little electric element inside the kettle heats up to a few hundred degrees instantly, giving you a nice hot cup of tea in just a few minutes.

Instead, we congregate in the wee hours of the morning, groggy and hung over, cursing our dumb luck for being the chosen crew to start up the engine room. If you talk to anyone else in the Navy (or the rest of the armed services) who understands what a nuc is, you will typically hear that we chose this life and we

---

14. Yes, that is a good thing. As in, "It's critical that the plant operate properly before we get underway!"

knew what we were getting into. Not only that, but we get advanced faster and get paid more, so we should shut up and stop bitching.

That's only half true. None of us really knew what we were signing up for when we signed on the dotted line. I had dreams of sailing to Australia and being welcomed with open arms by busty Australian blondes eager to make an American sailor happy! At least that was what was sold to me when I enlisted in the Navy.

The truth is that when we did finally get to Australia, which was a one-time occurrence, we had only about seventy-two hours total in port, and twenty-four of those hours were spent on the boat in a duty rotation. Being one of the junior personnel at the time, I got the extreme pleasure of being involved in every single startup until I was fully qualified to stand my own watches.

This meant showing up at 3 AM with very little sleep and having missed out on all those supposed beauties somewhere in Perth. Instead, I was hanging out in the lower ass end of the ship with my buddy Tom watching a single pressure gauge, waiting for something to happen.

When the 2MC rang out with the orders, I thought we were going to spring into action and start doing something. However, when you hang out in the lower bowels of the ship, not very much happens. Every now and then the supervisor would come down and make sure we weren't sleeping, but otherwise there wasn't much to do for some time.

Later in my career, I found out there actually was a great deal going on and was proud to say that I knew how to start up the entire reactor plant and steam plant and knew everyone's job throughout the process. Everything from pulling rods and getting the reactor critical, to bringing steam down the header and getting the turbines online. All told, there are nearly 150 procedures that must be followed in sequence in order to bring a reactor online and get an engine room ready to get the ship underway.

"All right…now what?" I asked, eager to get things moving.

"Wait. Don't you know that's the Navy's motto? 'Hurry up and wait!'" Tom replied.

"Isn't there something we should be doing?" I needed a reason for being awake so damn early. That, and I needed something to keep me busy so I wouldn't just fall asleep on the one and only workout bench on the entire boat.

"Sure, go get the manuals and figure out how to get the main seawater plant started."[15]

Tom knew that I wasn't going to stop asking questions, and he figured that if I started reading about starting up a seawater system then I might just leave him alone and resume my watch—making sure that he didn't get caught with his hat over his eyes catching a cat-nap.

I grabbed the five-pound manual from the locker (a Navy term for shelf, cabinet, and, of course, locker) and opened the green plastic binder to the seawater system. The entire process was about five steps long: 1) open the valves, 2) wait for an order, 3) start the pumps, 4) make sure the pumps are running, and 5) take your logs.

Of course, that seems pretty straightforward and shouldn't take all that long. However, this was just one procedure among dozens of other procedures, all needing to happen at a precise time, in the right order, and only when certain criteria were met.

This is ultimately what you learn aboard a submarine—how to sequence everything!

Sequencing is so engrained in everything we did that we never really gave it much attention after a while. Just like night follows day, so too did one procedure follow after another, and another after that, and so on until everything was steady state.

---

15. Typical sailor response…go figure it out your damn self!

Each sequence must happen in the right order once the underlying prerequisites are met in order for a system to operate correctly. If done out of order or when the requirements aren't met, you can create disastrous results. On a submarine, that can mean millions of dollars of damage, serious injury, or a potential nuclear reactor failure! (We don't say "meltdown" because the odds of actually melting a nuclear reactor's core, especially in a ship designed to sink, is damn near impossible unless you are intentionally trying to break it!)

The challenge that I see most business owners facing is that they don't have procedures in place for almost anything, which means that their sequences are either nonexistent or erratic at best. However, as I've mentioned previously, a business is nothing more than a series of systems designed to achieve a common goal. Systems comprise processes and procedures, each of which must be carried out in the correct sequence to achieve the desired result.

It's just like baking a cake: Cook all the ingredients before you mix them up properly, and you'll have baked eggs and smoke billowing out of the oven rather than the delicious chocolate aroma you were hoping for.

You need to create the right sequences to achieve the desired outcome. When you think of the desired outcome, you work backward and determine what the right sequence is, and which systems you must have in place. Luckily for you, I'm going to outline the right systems that you must have in place in order for your business to grow effectively.

Although these systems are listed in their order of importance, the failure to have any one of these in place will result in less than desirable results, or a complete business failure.

Here are the core systems you must have in your business to help you succeed:

Most people in business will argue that this is not a complete overview of a business, but as you read on and learn about each of these systems, the processes and procedures you must follow in each, and how they all relate back to the overall business, I think you will begin to see why these systems are so vital to the continued success of any organization.

I will further explain how even the biggest companies in the world are using these same systems to ensure continued growth and longevity, even though they don't call them by these names specifically.

You, as the CEO, owner, or entrepreneur, need to understand all these systems and components, but you don't need to be the expert in each. Instead, you need to be the leader and overseer of the systems and make sure that your people are working through each system as you have designed it.[16]

Just as when I was starting out in the bottom of the engine room I didn't know all of what was going on elsewhere, so too will your employees be wondering why the hell you are setting certain practices in stone and forcing compliance.

---

16. In many cases, it's better if you don't know too much. The dumber you are (or act) as a leader, the more forgiving people are when you start asking the so-called "obvious" questions. Only then will you find out that some people don't actually know what they're doing.

When you're at the bottom of the ship looking around, your sight is limited to whatever is six feet in front of your eyes, and you don't know or care what is happening on the bridge. However, if you're at the top looking out at the horizon, you better damn well know and be comfortable with what is going on below to get you there.

Chapter Six
Marketing & Sales Uranium

According to Wikipedia (since I can't tell you what I know specifically), the Navy uses highly enriched uranium as its fuel for the nuclear power plant. This highly enriched uranium undergoes a fission reaction that produces extreme amounts of heat in the reactor core. That heat is transferred to the pressurized water in the core to create a very high temperature water loop that both cools the reactor and heats the secondary loop via a "steam generator" (Campbell 2017). This steam generated in the steam generator is sent to the engine room to spin four turbines: two for propulsion and two for electrical power generation.

Most people get naval reactors confused with nuclear bombs by referring to them as *fusion* reactors—they're not. We haven't figured out a way to harness cold fusion for power production—yet.[17]

Without the discovery of nuclear fission in the mid-1900s, there would likely be no nuclear-powered submarines or ships of any type for that matter. All large navy vessels would still be utilizing boilers, gas turbines, diesel generators, and huge battery compartments to keep them moving. Since a naval nuclear reactor is powered with highly enriched uranium, it doesn't require any refueling for the life of the vessel—something you can't say about any diesel boat.

---

17. Actually, there are research facilities that claim to have figured this out, but the risks are still pretty great. Maybe someday this incredible energy will be harnessed to solve all of our energy needs and maybe space travel too!

Just like uranium is the core of the submarine's ability to create steam, electricity, propulsion, and even potable water, so too is marketing the ultimate fuel for your business.

But most people approach marketing as if it were advertising—it isn't. These two words are not interchangeable, and you should stop using them that way right now.

Marketing is, by definition, "the activity, set of institutions, and processes for creating, communicating, delivering, and exchanging offerings that have value for customers, clients, partners, and society at large" (American Marketing Association, 2013). Advertising, on the other hand, is "the act or practice of calling public attention to one's product, service, need, etc., especially by paid announcements in newspapers and magazines, over radio or television, on billboards, etc." (Dictionary.com n.d.).

The difference here is that marketing is a process—a system designed to create value and ultimately produce results. Advertising is just a piece of the marketing system.

And yes, marketing is a system. Just like any other system, it has a process, a procedure, a formula that when applied correctly will result in an outcome that can be quantified, measured, repeated, and/or improved. Most companies conduct advertising as a one-off approach to potentially get new business.

Smart business owners approach marketing as a process, set it up like a system, manage it as a system, generate procedures around it, and are vigilant in following the system to maximum effectiveness. A marketing system is designed to continuously fuel your business with new prospects and customers using a variety of strategies and tactics. It is designed to create a "cash now, cash later, and cash flow" environment that will continue your growth.

A marketing system does three core things:

1. Attracts the right prospects to your business.

2. Converts those prospects to paying customers.

3. Retains those customers for the long term, creating a relationship with a client.

If you do not have a marketing system in place, at best you can hope to get new customers by dumb luck or one-off advertising efforts. Marketing builds upon itself to create a relationship with your customers so you don't have to worry about where the next customer is coming from.

I use the term FOCUS to remind me how to create a system for marketing. Here is my Six-part FOCUS Formula for creating a marketing system:

F – Fill a (hidden) need your prospect has

O – Offer them something of incredible value that

C – Changes their reality using your

U – Unique value proposition so that you can implement

S – Systems that allow you to scale your business.

I developed my FOCUS Formula[18] as I continued to help entrepreneurs and business owners figure out how to turn their ideas into actual businesses they could scale. What I found was that people kept selling the "thing" they created or wanted to create, rather than selling the outcome of whatever that thing was.

In order to create desire in a prospect that moves them to action (opting in, buying, coming back, etc.), you must FOCUS on them—their needs and desires. Once you do that, you create the "thing," whatever IT is, to satisfy that need and desire, and you sell them that via a system.

---

18. If you haven't received a copy yet, visit www.AngelNetwork.com/bonus to get a free video course, special report, and of course the FOCUS Formula!

Your unique value proposition is what you use to sell your thing. Dan Kennedy refers to the selling side of the value proposition as the "Unique Selling Proposition" and explains it thus: "Why should I, your ideal prospect, choose to do business with you over and above any other option in the marketplace, including doing nothing?" (Kennedy 2006).

Now, this book isn't focused on the selling and marketing framework, but on how to create a system that helps you grow your business. If you want to learn more about creating marketing and advertising materials, I suggest you pick up everything Dan Kennedy has ever written and subscribe to his monthly newsletter at www.nobsinnercircle.com.[19]

However, I will show you what is referred to as a marketing "funnel" that utilizes the principles found in every successful company's marketing system. The funnel is an illustration of a value ladder that helps you create an ongoing customer relationship and escalated sales process for each of your products and services. If you have only one product or service, you are at risk of being copied or viewed as a commodity as others will likely compete with you on price (assuming you're successful), and that is a game with no winners.

---

19. I am not being paid to endorse Dan Kennedy, NO B.S. INNER CIRCLE, or any other organization in this book. I have no affiliation with Dan other than being a newsletter subscriber, nor did I receive any form of compensation for this endorsement.

The only real way to grow a business is through successful acquisition of new customers at a profit, in an ongoing manner, and by creating a higher lifetime customer value than your competitors. This is done through a complete and thorough marketing funnel, as illustrated here:

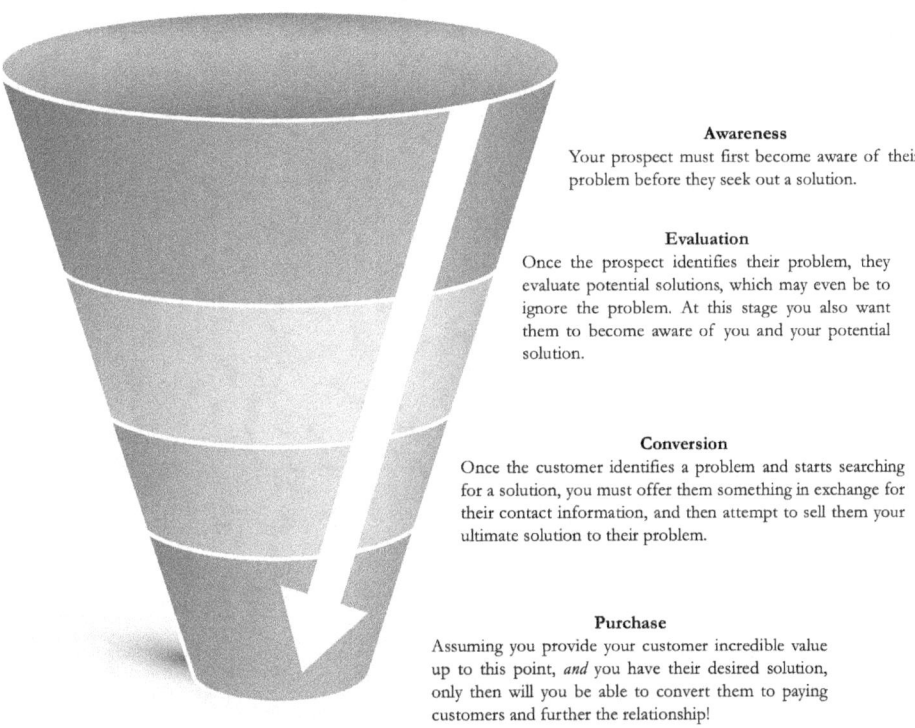

Awareness
Your prospect must first become aware of their problem before they seek out a solution.

Evaluation
Once the prospect identifies their problem, they evaluate potential solutions, which may even be to ignore the problem. At this stage you also want them to become aware of you and your potential solution.

Conversion
Once the customer identifies a problem and starts searching for a solution, you must offer them something in exchange for their contact information, and then attempt to sell them your ultimate solution to their problem.

Purchase
Assuming you provide your customer incredible value up to this point, *and* you have their desired solution, only then will you be able to convert them to paying customers and further the relationship!

The trick here is to have an ongoing or "evergreen" funnel so you aren't just creating a one-time sale but rather an ongoing revenue stream that will keep your customers coming back time and again. Or better yet, they pay you on a regular basis for a service that doesn't require additional man-hours.

This is how you scale a business: when you uncouple yourself and your team from the "payment per unit of time," or "hours for dollars" dilemma.[20] Once you have done that, created a product or service that doesn't require more time

---

20. Put another way, un-fuck yourself and your business will grow. Too harsh? Must have hit a nerve then...

and effort for each additional sale you make, and created a system for bringing in more customers on a daily basis, then you have truly created a scalable business!

Of course, to continue this growth, you must be able to service all those customers, which is the second most important system you must create.

Chapter Seven
Operation: Customer Service Excellence

"Three knots to nowhere" is a common term in the engine room of a submarine. When you are in a black tube with no windows, no maps, no TVs, and no sense of where you are, you don't really get the sensation you are going anywhere. When the same lights on the control panels stay illuminated for the 30+ day runs without coming up above the ocean's waves, and the needles on the gauges never move more than a gnat's ass in one direction or another, you get the odd sensation that someone is playing a cruel *Groundhog Day* type of joke on you.

The seafoam-green painted bilges beginning to collect dust and oil are the only indication that time is actually moving forward. The world seems to come to a standstill in the engine room. The turbines hum along at 3600 RPM giving off a rhythmic purr, and the only changes in the acoustics happen on the midnight watch when the oil filters are cleaned and pumps are cycled. Otherwise, time stops.

You get a false sense of security when nothing changes for weeks or months on end. No new bells are rung up, and you tend to forget that the pipe three inches from your head contains hundreds of pounds of superheated steam racing along at supersonic speeds.

So when the 1MC ship-wide speaker system sounded with the captain's panic-stricken voice, "Emergency Deep! Maneuvering, all ahead—flank cavitate!" we nearly shit ourselves![21]

This type of bell is one that only sounds in Hollywood movies or as a joke when you're trying to rack someone out[22] at O-dark thirty!

Suddenly, the ship made a nosedive down, and the sound of the turbines picking up speed reminded us of the awesome power of the steam inside those silver pipes. The pumps were kicked on into high gear, and we all braced as the boat angled further and further down, as if we were searching for Davy Jones himself!

The funny thing about being on a submarine is that you are always cleaning something.

"If you have time to lean, you have time to clean!" is a favorite saying among the chiefs.

You would think that between every crewmember cleaning his area on a regular basis and the Friday morning "Field Days" (not to be confused with fun-filled school-type field days) where all hands pitch in to shine pipes, vacuum dust bunnies, and scrub the decks, somehow all the dirt, oil, and filth would be minimal. You would only think that until you are involved in an emergency maneuver or a severe sea state where the boat conducts sixty-degree rolls from one side to the other, or a downward angle like we were experiencing just then.

---

21. People always ask me if I was afraid on a submarine. "What's it like?" they ask…It's like locking yourself in a storage container with almost no ventilation, no windows, no sunlight, bad food, coffee that tastes like shitty water, and a bunch of raunchy other guys, and all we do is stare at dials and gauges most of the time. However, when you hear a random order of the highest order, your adrenaline takes you from sound asleep to half-crazed lunatic with a purpose in two seconds flat!

22 "Racking someone out" is the same as getting them out of bed. However, on a submarine, nothing is done with grace, so instead of nudging your buddy to wake up, you shine the brightest damn flashlight you can in their eyes and yell in their ear. The reaction is priceless…unless you get too close and their reaction is to sock you in the face!

On those occasions, you learn just how recessed some of those hidden areas are when dirt, oil, water, and unsecured loads come flying from every conceivable direction. Every loose item is "rigged for dive" upon initially embarking on your voyage, but things shake loose, and people tend to forget to secure lockers and loads on occasion. During this deep dive, I witnessed a fifty-five-pound dumbbell set skid along the deck and ram directly into a massive oil tank twenty feet away with a thunderous CLANG, and the adjustable weights flew across the engine room.

Oil was spilling from the overheads and wires appeared to be bleeding the golden-brown liquid in every direction!

After what seemed like an hour of this high-speed maneuvering, we leveled off and rang up "All ahead standard" to level out several hundred feet lower from where we had originally begun.

Apparently, the Officer of the Deck (OOD) miscalculated his course during a recent turn and had us headed straight for a merchant cargo carrier that would have ripped us in two like a small toothpick!

Upon turning the periscope back in the direction we were headed, the ship was far closer than anticipated and bearing down fast!

To survive the ordeal, we needed to go deep…FAST!

In those few seconds, everything that we had been trained for, and every one of our systems, needed to be called upon and relied on as a matter of life and death. Without the training and our systems working properly, we could have easily been another ill-fated war story.

Luckily for you, most business owners don't experience such dire situations where their crew faces life and death decisions. Luckily for us, we knew what we were doing, and our systems were designed to handle that type of situation.

An operation means many things to different people. In the Navy, an operation is a set of procedures and processes carried out to achieve an objective. Think SEAL Team 6 extracting Bin Laden—one core objective that must be achieved and all the steps that must happen in order to make that happen.

In business, most people consider "Operations" as something that you do daily to simply get the job done. Many would equate it to a manufacturing process—to them, that is an operational system.

However, when I discuss an operational system for your business, it is much deeper than that, though the objective is actually very simple:

CUSTOMER SERVICE EXCELLENCE

Operations is simply delivering the promises you made in your marketing and sales material to the customer in the way *they* expect you to.[23] It is providing the ultimate experience to your customer so that they have an answer to the question we asked in the beginning:

"Why should I do business with you, over and above any other option available to me, including doing nothing?"

In short, operations are an extension of marketing and sales. Operational systems should all be geared toward this one common goal.

Of course, that begs the question, "How do you create a *system* that services the customer in such a way that they are reluctant to seek out goods, services, or products in your category from any other competitor, real or imagined?"

This is where we must look back at both naval operations systems and manufacturing systems.

---

23. In other words, service delivery. Your entire business lives and dies on how well you manage this process of giving the customer what you promised when you sold him something.

In order to achieve operational excellence, and by virtue of this, customer service excellence, you must be 100 percent focused on the outcome *expected* by the customer.

Enter the **Theory of Constraints** (TOC). The theory of constraints states, quite simply, that there is one and only one limiting process at a time in any system that is preventing you from achieving this goal of customer service excellence.

This same theory is what spawned the **Toyota Production System (TPS)**, **Just In Time (JIT)** manufacturing, and is a very close partner to the **Lean & Six Sigma** manufacturing theories. There are several books focused on these specific topics, so I won't go into the complete details of each of these theories but will instead focus on how you can start to apply these principles, specifically focusing on service-based businesses rather than manufacturing.

CREATING AN OPERATING SYSTEM

An operations system should, at a bare minimum, achieve the following objectives:

1. Streamline the service delivery of a product or service from point of sale to completion.

2. Eliminate wasteful steps in every process that do not add value to the customer or the value chain itself.

3. Enhance the customer experience throughout the process.

4. Provide meaningful information back to the management team on how to improve the overall customer experience.

5. Be procedural and systemized.

6. Be repeatable.

7. Be scalable.

8. Move expertise upstream.

There are steps that every organization must make when implementing an operations system like this, and we will discuss each of these in detail to help you create a truly "lean" operations system that maximizes customer value.

However, for you to make this successful, you must first drink the Kool-Aid on this one premise:

Operational systems are merely extensions of sales & marketing efforts and are wholly designed to enhance customer value.[24]

In other words, if it doesn't add value from the customer's perspective, it doesn't matter how much you care for it—it doesn't make sense. In *Lean Thinking*, James Womack discusses an example from the airline industry. In that example, he lays out quite simply how different the perception of value is from the airline's view and the customer's (Womack 2002).

As a customer, you simply want to get from Point A to Point B as quickly as possible, safely, and with as little hassle as possible. However, the airline instead adds layovers and strange routes to satisfy their logistics requirements, while adding entertainment systems at each seat and airline lounges in hopes of making the experience "bearable." This doesn't really add value to us travelers from our point of view, and making something "bearable" should be just as sinful as not providing the service to begin with.

Now, assuming you are on board with making every step of your operations customer-facing…

---

24. Here's the deal—everyone should be furthering the sale of your products and services, and once the first sale is made, the operational side of the equation should be helping to make the next successive sale in your pipeline. If it isn't, then you're leaving money on the table and your customers will look for better alternatives.

And assuming you understand that by virtue of adding value at every turn it enhances the customer relationship…

And you buy into the fact that enhancing that relationship is key to retaining and earning more customers…

And you further agree that retaining existing customers is far cheaper, easier, and frankly better than trying to constantly find new customers…

Then we can move on with the building of an operations system to streamline, improve, and enhance your business in every conceivable way.

In order to make this chapter succinct, I will break down each one of the eight points made previously with as direct an example as I can in smaller chapters. I want to get the point across, but not at risk of losing you in mind-numbing details that will put you to sleep.

If you need further guidance on how to implement these systems, simply visit www.AngelNetwork.com for more in-depth examples and training.

Chapter Eight
Streamlining Service Delivery

So, number one and number two go hand in hand, but in the end, they are vital to the overall success of your operations system.

Aboard a submarine, the reactor compartment is in the middle of the ship. This means that the weapons, control room, sonar, and every other non-engineering application are separated by a nuclear reactor from the people powering and propelling the ship forward.

Unfortunately, however, the folks in the control room are the only ones who can see and know where the ship is going, how fast it must go, and what obstacles lie in its path. Therefore, the Officer of the Deck (OOD)[25] must be able to communicate directly with the Engineering Officer of the Watch (EOOW) in maneuvering to tell him what bell to ring up and what speed to move the ship forward.

For this reason, a communication method must be developed to relay information back and forth so that when the OOD (the customer) requests something, the EOOW and his team in maneuvering (the service provider) can provide the service in a timely and efficient manner.

One option, of course, is to have two-way radio communication, but that has the downside of radio interference and audio that can be lost in translation.

Another choice is a phone call using the 2JV communication system. That requires the OOD dialing up the number for maneuvering, ringing the bell on

---

25. Have you noticed yet how many TLAs there are in here? Yeah, sailors talk fast and think slow, so we need Three Letter Acronyms (TLAs) to help us out. We also don't just say the letters E-O-O-W, we'll say "eeeoww" to shorten up the four-letter acronyms.

the phone (think old-school dialing up the switchboard operator when phones were first invented), then having the EOOW pick up the phone and order the throttle man to open the throttles.

The silliest option might be a person who can run the message back and forth from the control room, down a ladder, through the mess decks, through a watertight door, up another ladder, into maneuvering, and then back when the bell has been met.[26]

Of course, that sounds ridiculous, but that is the way that most business owners actually run their businesses. They have inefficient processes that unnecessarily add steps to a procedure to complete a simple task. The goal is to get the customer their final product or service as quickly as possible with as little frustration as possible.

The Navy chose a much easier method. An analog "bell" that looks like an antique clock. The control room operator moves a needle to the desired bell, which then rings back on the throttle man's dashboard, and he then acknowledges receipt of the bell by moving his needle to match the desired bell, calling out the new speed to the EOOW.

Quick. Easy. Efficient. And everyone is happy because there aren't any unnecessary steps.

Your task is to look at what happens from the time your customer requests something, then every step in the process until they get the desired result. Does each step need to be there, and if so, why?

This leads to the next step in a good operational system.

---

26. A bell is a call for a new speed. Engine rooms are notoriously noisy, and were much more so on older vessels, so a device was designed to alert the engineman what speed was needed using an Engine Order Telegraph or EOT. The device is attached to a bell that clangs loud enough to be heard in even the noisiest engine rooms, and hence the speed being called is termed a "bell."

Chapter Nine
Eliminate Waste

The Japanese have a term for waste: *Muda*.

Muda is anything that is done that does not add value to your customer, again, from the customer's perspective, and instead detracts from the overall experience. You can find examples of waste everywhere you go, and it isn't hard.

Wasteful steps in a process may not seem like a big deal, but when you start thinking about scaling an operation, it becomes a huge issue.

One of the most wasteful things I see when working with any business is their chain of command process. Most business owners feel that they must be in control of almost every decision being made and, as a result, create major bottlenecks in their business that prevent them from growing.

A perfect example is in Timothy Ferriss's *The 4-Hour Work Week* wherein he discusses selling his supplements online and having a barrage of questions that kept coming back to him. Even after implementing a frequently asked questions (FAQ) process, he still received comments and complaints. In order to reduce or eliminate the bottleneck or constraint—his need to be the person making the decision—he implemented a simple rule: any request that resulted in less than a $500 cost to the company could be made by the customer service representative without any need to contact Tim (Ferriss 2006).

This one shift changed the constraint from him to another area of his business. This is exactly what the Theory of Constraints model does: moves the constraining or limiting process or task in your business to another area, thereby allowing you to increase capacity and provide a better overall customer experience. By eliminating the need to make the decisions for trivial items in his business, Ferriss was able to focus on growing the company rather than dealing with putting out all the fires.

Are you the limiting factor in your growth? Are you creating wasteful or otherwise hindering processes that could be improved or replaced?

Chapter Ten
Enhance the Customer Experience

In some cases, admittedly, it isn't possible to completely eliminate steps that are necessary to your service delivery. The previous airline example might be an example of that, but I have a better one that hopefully you can relate to.

Have you ever been to Disneyland? One of my favorite rides of all time is the Pirates of the Caribbean.

When I went with my family, we had to stand in line for what felt like hours. We didn't really want to stand in line for that long, but there wasn't much of an alternative if we wanted to go on the ride.

Well, actually there was.

I could have paid for an Express Pass that would have brought me near the front of the line almost instantly. There is also the mobile app that Disney has created specific to its theme parks that allows you to pay a nominal fee for the ability to get the fast passes even if you aren't in the vicinity of the ride you want a pass for. This isn't possible without the app and through purchasing the Max Pass. On a subsequent visit we purchased the Max Pass to the tune of $40 extra per day, and damned if it wasn't worth every penny. Just skipping the photo booth at the end of the day and getting all of our Disney photos digitally was worth the cost.

(There's another lesson in there for you—find a way to reward your best, highest paying customers whenever possible, and always try to get more of them!)

Given that I couldn't afford the express line the first time around, I noticed that Disney still took my situation into consideration. The entire line was an experience in and of itself. We were able to walk through the jungles, feel the mist that was coming from the stream, hear the laughter and songs of the pirates, and ultimately feel better about standing in line for so long.

Disney creates an experience for even the most frustrating processes. Disney also engineers their entire process for creating desire in their customers so they are less frustrated with the entire endeavor, and that is something worth keeping in mind when designing your customer experiences. Imagine if Disney ran the airline industry—how much better it would be!

Just imagine Goofy as your customer service/ticketing agent, Minnie as the flight attendant, and Yoda as the captain! How much better would that be?

Even in our chiropractic office we find little things that will enhance the customer experience to ensure customers appreciate coming in. As an example, we have proceduralized the greetings. From the phone script to the greeting the patients receive upon walking in the door the first time, we choreograph as much as possible. Patients who come in regularly have their coffee or tea ready for them when they arrive, and newcomers are welcomed with a beautiful office, essential oils, and fresh fruit with the health benefits listed for their convenience.

These may all be little and trivial to you, but I would bet almost none of your competitors are doing it, so why not try it out? How can you increase the customer experience and add value to your processes?

Chapter Eleven
Provide Meaningful Feedback

Earlier I discussed how you might be the constraint holding your business back from growing, but I don't want you to think that you should be removed from the equation altogether.

"Trust, but verify" was Reagan's saying.

You too, as the CEO, owner, or executive, must do the same thing, but how? Especially in a multilayered, even multinational organization, how do you know your business is operating the right way?

There must be key performance indicators that, and this is important, are directly related to the overall customer experience!

Most managers and business owners focus on metrics that are purely financial in nature.

"Amount of revenue per cash register" or "Number of sales per sales representative."

These are okay, and in some cases necessary, but they aren't necessarily directly attributable to customer satisfaction.

Instead, you want to focus first on the customer and what the customer sees as value before you begin creating metrics for your employees to meet.

In one of the businesses I worked with, one of the metrics was "time per inspection"; this was a key metric along with "percentage of completed work."

Unfortunately, it didn't really fit into the company's overall value of putting quality work first. Imagine how happy you would be if you went to a high-end dealer to service your Lexus or Range Rover and the mechanics were incentivized to get the job done as quickly as they could to get onto the next car!

In that situation, speed and efficiency aren't necessarily the top concern.

However, at McDonald's where you have a screaming toddler in the back seat waiting for a Happy Meal, the already drained parent is counting the seconds it takes to get to the window in order to shut the young one up! In that case, time spent in line per customer would be a good metric.

The key is to focus first on what the customer values, then create metrics around those. Then, what you do is implement a dashboard or reporting system that gives you, weekly if not daily, an update on all the key metrics that drive growth in your business.

In recent times, the Net Promoter Score (NPS) has been developed to provide you with a very simple way to determine if you are providing your customers with the level of service *they* desire. Just because you think that what you do is important doesn't mean that it is what the customer values.

Another example is going to the doctor's office. A customer doesn't want to waste their time at the doctor's office, but so many doctors equate this to a rapid-fire exam and diagnosis of the problem.

What results is a patient sitting in the waiting room for three, five, even ten times longer than they spend with the doctor, and they are displeased with the overall experience. Instead, what a patient wants is a shorter stay in the waiting room and a longer time with the person they are actually paying to see. They want a thorough diagnosis without a lengthy waste of time twiddling their thumbs hoping to get their issue resolved soon.

Think of what metrics you need to keep an eye on that will indicate whether your customers are happy with your service.

How do you figure out what the customers want?

Just ASK!

Chapter Twelve
Create a Procedure

The hottest day of my life happened while "playing pretend." That's what Tom liked to call it when we ran drills.

"Just a bunch of grown-ass men playing pretend with millions of dollars of equipment and a nuclear bomb down the hall!"

There I was standing in my steam suit, sweating bullets and laughing because, in all honesty, he was right. We were playing pretend.

Just moments earlier we heard the 1MC announcement, "Steam line rupture in the engine room. Off going watch, conduct immediate action procedures."

That was all I needed to hear. As the off going (meaning just relieved) engine room supervisor, it was my job to get into a steam suit and get back to isolate the leak, hopefully saving the crew from certain death.

Of course this was a drill, so I could laugh a little at the situation.

A steam line rupture is one of three absolutely deadly accidents that could occur on a submarine and admittedly the scariest for anyone in the engine room. A simple one-inch crack in a high-pressure steam line could result in the deaths of everyone in the engine room within three minutes.

Temperatures would soar over 200 degrees Fahrenheit, and the pressure buildup would happen so fast that your eardrums would burst and cause massive bleeding. Without immediate isolation, all personnel in the engine room would suffer a grim fate, and it wasn't something to be taken lightly.

Luckily, or more importantly, by design, there haven't been any steam line ruptures in the history of nuclear submarines.

However, we still trained.

A steam suit is designed to keep the heat out as much as possible and provide positive pressure, thus preventing steam from getting inside the suit. It's a silver, full-body suit that harkens back to the 1960s space movies, and looks just as goofy and clumsy as they did on TV.

Every few feet, you hook your steam suit into an emergency air manifold to provide pressure inside the suit and some airflow. This kept the person wearing the suit alive while they were inside a steam-filled compartment with zero visibility.

The job of the person wearing the suit was to identify the leak, isolate it, and if not already done, shut down the entire steam plant to prevent a catastrophic loss of life and equipment. To do this meant memorizing and understanding countless procedures and diagrams, which is why the senior mechanic not on watch was designated as the person to head into the engine room.

There I was, going from one manifold to the next, feeling my way through the engine room because I had a semi-transparent film placed on my hood the moment I entered the engine room. The air conditioning had shut off as part of the drill, and the temperature in the space was over 120 degrees Fahrenheit. The temperature in the suit was likely higher than that. The little airflow I had wasn't enough to keep my face mask from fogging up nor enough to keep sweat from dripping into my eyes.

"Okay," I thought to myself, "Listen for the noise."

You had to keep walking through the procedure in your head, one that you had memorized time and again because there was no referencing a manual at this point.

I heard the noise in the lower compartment, and carefully but quickly made my way there. The sweat continued to drip down my face, and I could feel my shirt getting wetter and wetter.

At one point, it became incredibly hard to breathe, and I struggled to find the next manifold to plug into. You didn't get fresh oxygen in the suit if you didn't plug your air hose into a manifold, and doing this with very little light and almost no visibility was difficult at best. If you've ever been punched in the stomach and had the wind knocked out of you while trying to swim underwater, you might know what that feeling was for me.

I wanted to rip the suit off and take a giant breath, but that wouldn't help those who were relying on me, and it would make me look foolish, weak, and inexperienced. That wasn't going to happen.

I fumbled around and found the manifold, and, with my giant Stay Puft Marshmallow Man gloves on, managed to plug into the manifold and take a giant breath.

"Okay, deep breath. Now, isolate the leak."

I had to keep reminding myself that there were others counting on me. Even though it was a drill, what if I were ever in this situation? Would I want to freeze and let others down? No. I wouldn't.

I knew the systems by heart and knew there were two valves I could shut (we don't use the term "close" in the Navy) to help isolate the leak.

After finding them and painstakingly shutting the valves, the sound of steam hissing out slowed but didn't stop. There was another valve going into the reactor compartment that I knew needed to be shut to fully isolate the leak.

Again, fumbling in the dark and the Sahara Desert heat, I found the valve and turned it, one rotation after another, and managed to shut the valve and isolate the leak.

"Next step, contact the Conn and inform them of the situation."

I found the nearest phone, rang the control room, and unplugged the hose from the manifold. I needed it to be as quiet as possible so they could understand me through my mask, and the ventilation into the suit would make it sound like someone trying to talk on a cell phone in high winds.

"The leak is secured. Repeat, the steam leak is secured in Engine Room Forward!" I blurted as loud as I could.

Now, to wait.

"Steam line rupture is secure. Ventilating the engine room," came the garbled voice over the 1MC sound system.

I headed back to the tunnel leading toward the forward compartment where the only thing saving the rest of the crew was a watertight hatch. Once the steam was sucked out of the engine room through our ventilation system, my job was to ensure the compartment was safe prior to allowing other personnel in for assistance.

I instantly felt a massive pressure change when the ventilation began; my ears popped abruptly, and damn that hurt! Once in the tunnel, I positioned myself by the hatch, watching the pressure gauge in the engine room slowly return to normal as the "steam" was sucked out of the compartment and out to the atmosphere beyond the hull.

Once the pressure normalized, I opened the hatch, and the crew entered in immediately to complete the rest of the action steps in the procedure. They helped me doff (remove) my gear, allowing me to breathe freely.

I was dripping wet with sweat and stank like a pig in manure, but I was finally cooling down. I had completed the action steps in the correct order and, theoretically, saved the rest of the crew.

If it wasn't for having a procedure and then committing that procedure to memory, I would never have been able to pull all of that off in under five minutes like I did.

All of us knew that there was a trigger mechanism that kicked off a series of events, which led to the successful resolution of a major problem. In most cases, the problem isn't as severe as near-certain death, but the fact remains that without clear, well-defined and thought-out procedures, successful resolution is hit or miss at best.

Another huge mistake most business owners make is that they don't turn their processes into written procedures. They assume that by training their staff on it once or twice, everything is getting done correctly every time.

This is the worst possible assumption you could make about your business. If you think that *telling* someone how to do something is enough, you're delusional.

Instead, you need to focus on demonstrating, training, documenting, and then verifying compliance with your procedures. A process is only a process inasmuch as people follow it religiously.

When we started up our $30 million turbine using high-pressure steam, we didn't "wing it" and hope that we were all on the same page and getting everything done in sequence.

We had multivolume procedures designed to get it right every single time. The challenge of trying to simply start up a multimillion-dollar system with thousands of moving parts is that one person alone couldn't do it. Not effectively, anyway.

Instead, you need a team to make the magic happen. In order for team members to always be on the same page, there must first be a page to get on. A procedure must be written down, documented, and reviewed by everyone to make sure it makes sense.

Bringing saturated steam—that is, steam with water droplets in it—screaming hundreds of feet per second down a steel header and expecting that moisture to make a sixty-degree turn down to the turbines and not cause any damage is a really bad idea. To ensure that doesn't happen, you must first get the steam superheated and drain any and all moisture out of the pipes slowly before you just fling open the stop valves. This is something that is done with care and patience, and when someone tries to rush through it, everyone knows they did because it sounds like someone's popping off .22 caliber bullets against a metal wall!

Procedures don't only save time, they also save equipment, money, and lives. SEAL teams don't rush into a building trying to subdue enemy combatants without having a very well detailed plan on how to enter, along with standard procedures they follow before, during, and after entry. Careless operations lead to sloppy results, and sloppy results can end up with dire, even mortal consequences.

When I was tasked with developing a mobile technology game plan for the 400+ remote field staff in our company, I didn't start with a blank canvas. We already had procedures in place for how the field operated on a daily basis, though it was disjointed and in complete disarray at times.

The goal of moving forward with advanced technology was threefold:

1. Optimize
2. Innovate
3. Transform

First, we needed to optimize what was already happening in the field. An inspector in New York City should have a similar if not identical plan for how to engage and work with customers as does the inspector in Montana, Florida, or Alaska. This was an unpopular idea to say the least because everyone felt that they had a unique geography, unique customers, and unique operating procedures.

Truth be told, there were variances, but these variances were minimal compared to the drastic differences everyone thought they had. We identified the core components that every person must follow when working in the field with a customer and developed a standard operating procedure (SOP) for the majority of our staff that could be used without change.

This idea, though unpopular, proved beneficial because it highlighted key areas where staff could improve. It also showed management the areas where they had neglected to provide proper training and communication, which is vital to the success of the organization. Writing down the SOPs and having others review them led to advanced communication and a better overall customer experience.

Second, we had to innovate how we did things. With our company being 150 years old and segmented in so many areas, there was a vast amount of information, experience, and knowledge from which to draw insights and get help. However, most of the staff had neither the awareness of these resources nor the inclination to ask for help should they need it.

There was already too much to do and too little time. However, by optimizing processes, we could free up at least two hours per week per person in the field. This may not seem like much, but given how little time the staff had to perform their duties already, this really added up. Instead of taking that time and just trying to plug it with more work, we suggested that the staff spend more time with customers, provide a better overall experience, and increase the perceived value of the company.

Everyone liked this idea, and it ultimately helped the brand image and company. Now we had mobile technology in the hands of our staff, and they could use that technology to provide better service to our customers.

What we did next was identify all the resources available to our staff and customers online that we had fully utilized. We found a way to make the processes, procedures, and resources universally available on-demand, thus reducing and eliminating costly mistakes and inefficiencies. This was immediately received by the staff as a big win, and the customers loved getting better service as well.

Finally, transformation. Transforming an organization of any size is challenging, but a multinational conglomerate becomes especially difficult. However, because of optimizing and innovating our existing processes, we found that we were able to gather more data and create better insights for our decision-makers in corporate.

Additionally, now that the staff was getting familiar with the baseline level of technology, we could begin to explore new technology that was on the fringe without having much pushback. Adding additional software to their mobile devices, as well as accessories that normally required separate equipment, such as borescopes, infrared cameras, smart glasses, remote visual assistance, and even drones, gave us an even greater advantage over the competition and helped secure our position as the industry leader.

None of that could have happened without first writing down the procedures as they were or the goals they aimed to achieve. Once written down, the procedures could be added to, modified, or amended as needed in smaller steps rather than having to make a complete overhaul. This led to further innovation and customer satisfaction.

The process of documenting a procedure doesn't need to be hard, either. Giving your employees an opportunity to do something of value to the organization is enough to motivate some to take up the task. Start by just making a list of everything they do for one task, and then spend some time diving deeper into that with them.

If you do this, I promise you will initially be biting your tongue and holding back fits of rage as you hear your employees recite the most lackadaisical, nonchalant, lazy, and incomplete processes you could imagine for even the most basic things…like answering the phone.

Once it is written down, simply refine what needs to be refined and modify it to make it succinct and simple so anyone can follow it. Then, you turn it into a system that others can follow. If you find there is something that can be automated in the process, feel free to do so, but make sure it follows the cardinal rule: **automation must add value from the customer's perspective.**

Bottom line, if it isn't written down, your staff won't follow through and do what you want them to do the same way every time.

Having a standard operating procedure or SOP in your business may not save your life, but it could save your business!

Chapter Thirteen
Make It Repeatable

When you create a process and a system, it should automatically be repeatable. Think of McDonald's with the pimple-faced teenager (or now the "overworked and underpaid" millennial) who can somehow manage to get the order right 90 percent of the time without much more motivation than a cow with its face already in the trough.

The reason that they can get it right is because the system boils down every step to the simplest task possible so that it can be repeated time and again without fail.

This means your procedures aren't novels.

They are one instruction per line, and as simple as you can make it so that others can follow along easily.

When we started up any system on the ship, we would have something like:

> Step 1. Open Valve A.
>
> Step 2. Turn the pump switch from "Off" to "On."
>
> Step 3. Check that the pressure gauge indicates flow.

Now mind you, we were very highly trained, and you wouldn't think you would need this level of granularity. In some cases, it seemed comical. Most of us could start up the engine room from memory, blindfolded, with one hand tied behind our back. But that's because we had followed the procedure so many times it was second nature. This is what happens when you have solid procedures and systems in place—things happen automatically and correctly.

But here's the thing—if it isn't comically easy to you, then it won't be easily repeated by your staff. This isn't to say that they aren't smart or capable. Instead, you allow them to take their eyes off the procedure for more than half a second, get the task completed, and then go back and find where they left off.

Writing a procedure with five tasks in one paragraph is almost guaranteeing that the process won't be repeated the right way every time. Instead, focus on short, sweet bullet points that can be easily followed.

You could also create a flow chart full of "If/Then" or "Yes/No" decision points that will help your staff answer questions themselves without needing management support for the most basic items. In *The 4-Hour Work Week*, Tim Ferriss described how he was constantly barraged by his customer service reps who needed to come to him for every decision involving a customer question or complaint.

To alleviate that stress and strain on himself personally, Ferriss devised a simple script for agents to follow, a flow chart of how to handle complaints, and a maximum threshold that an agent could automatically act on. By putting these in place, he diminished questions to him personally by over 90 percent. This is how you free up your time!

What processes do you have in place that could be made simpler, and therefore repeatable?

Chapter Fourteen
Make It Scalable

Here is the Holy Grail of any business owner, entrepreneur, or CEO—you want to be able to scale your business without additional headaches. You want more customers, more revenue, more profits, and fewer pains in your ass, right?

How do you make that happen?

First by identifying ways to make your customer happy, then creating systems and processes that support that, measuring and monitoring with meaningful KPIs, and then making the process simple to scale.

Most business owners are kidding themselves when they say things like, "The reason I can't grow is because my staff can't do their job right,"

Or…

"No one knows how to do this as well as I do, so I can't grow any more than I already have."

Bullshit.

Every single one of these systems is scalable if you follow the process properly.

Starting first with your marketing system. Here again we come back to the theory of constraints. Most businesses don't fail from a bad communication system. Some fail from poor operations, or they aren't innovative and get left behind.

Most, however, fail from not having a scalable, repeatable, verifiable marketing system in place.

This is the first system, of course, because it's the most important to getting sales and then growing. Operations is an extension of that process, and the theory of constraints helps us in this endeavor.

For example, when any business is starting out, their first challenge is getting customers. To do this you begin some sort of marketing campaign, whether online or off, and then find a process that works.

You then nail down that process, write it down, train someone else on it, and hand it off so you can focus on the next important piece: customer service excellence.

The initial constraint is no customer flow. Solve that problem, and your next challenge is service delivery. From there, you focus on streamlining your products and services and providing a great experience in the process.

The cycle then goes back to square one, where you expand your marketing reach or channels because now your capacity (ability to service your customers) has outgrown your customer base.

It's a virtuous cycle that continues if you realize that the constraint keeps changing, and you must keep identifying the constraint and removing it, then moving on to the next one.

That is how you scale. You remove the constraint, maximize the next constraint, then remove it and move to the next one. Maximizing the constraint simply means pushing it to its limit to find out what the limits are and then thinking creatively on how to remove that step as the constraint.

Most owners focus on simply putting out the fire of the day instead of focusing on growth.

How can you, after all, if there are constantly fires to put out?

Therefore, the last and final step in any operational system is key to the overall growth of your company. Before we get there, though, ask yourself:

"What is the one thing that, if completely overcome today, would allow me to grow more tomorrow?"

Answer this question honestly and objectively by looking at where the bottlenecks are in your entire value stream, and you will be well on your way to scaling your business.

Chapter Fifteen
Move the Expertise Upstream

Prior to Henry Ford creating the assembly line for cars, people who were building cars were experts in the entire process: design, production, construction, maintenance, and (supposedly) even sales.

This was a clunky process that was not scalable in any sense. It required one person to spend ample time on each step of the process to create one vehicle. If that person was sick or wanted to take vacation, no one else could simply step in and pick up where he left off.

This is exactly why we are driving Fords instead of Stanley Steamers (well, that and the fact that internal combustion engines were better suited for smaller vehicles).

When you think about building a car now, it seems silly to have one person building the whole thing. In fact, with 3D printing, robotics, automation, and ever-expanding technology, it almost seems silly to have people involved in any aspect of the production of a car these days.

However, take that same principle and apply it to your business. Are you the owner, operator, cashier, receptionist, appointment setter, salesperson, closer, and practitioner of your thing?

The best example I've come across are the neuro- and cardio-thoracic surgeons. These doctors are at the top of the "food chain," if you will, and only operate at the top. They are not scheduling patients, accepting copays, calling insurance companies, or dealing with anything else that can be handled by someone else.

They are focused only on their area of expertise, and they do it incredibly well. This is also why they are some of the highest-paid individuals in the medical field. The only people paid more are the owners of hospitals who have figured out how to amass enough of these experts to have an entire system for helping patients.

This too is why every other aspect of your operations system must be put in place—to move you up the chain of your business. The captain of a submarine is tasked with hundreds if not thousands of daily decisions in the operation of his ship and crew. Thus, he relies heavily on the systems in place, the procedures that are part of those systems, and the crew following the procedures to help him make those important and life-preserving decisions.

The captain will, at times, chastise someone for not properly cleaning a valve or a pipe because he knows that if the procedure for keeping equipment operational is not being followed as it should (and yes, there is a program for keeping valves clean), then other procedures could be impacted, which could eventually result in his inability to fulfill his mission and bring his crew home safely.

Again, this is a major misunderstanding of so many business owners and CEOs. They forget that their position is at the helm of the ship, making the vital decisions to keep the ship moving forward ahead of the competition. Thus, they spend their time focusing on minutiae that can easily be handled by someone else.

Why do they do this?

A few reasons, but the main one is that they don't trust it will get done to their specifications in a timely and efficient manner.

Why?

They have no systems, processes, or procedures in place that they can be assured their staff will follow to take care of any problems before they arise.

As a result, they constantly worry about whether the trash was taken out, the statements were mailed out properly, bills were paid, or even if payroll will be taken care of.

It's due to a lack of proper systems that the people who are meant to be the leaders cannot effectively lead. Their minds are so preoccupied with problems that keep coming up that they cannot spend time focusing on the future or the growth of their company.

To truly spend time focusing on the growth of your company, you must implement processes, procedures, and systems to handle the bulk of your operations and then find the right people to manage those systems. This gives you an opportunity to lead people the way you want to and empower them to make decisions that you know are in the best interests of the company.

You know this because you are the one who made sure the systems were set up correctly in the first place.

Remember: trust, but verify.

Now, do you have your operations system or outline in place? If not, get your best employee to start working with you on this right now!

Remember, exceptional operations mean exceptional customer experiences, which equate to repeat business and better word of mouth advertising and referrals.

Having a great operations system in place is the key to growing any business, big or small, tech or old-school. Whether you think you are making the next Facebook or simply running a multimillion-dollar cement business, having an operations system in place is vital to growing your business.

There's a reason Zuckerberg brought in Sheryl Sandberg to run Facebook—he knew that having the right person creating a streamlined operation was the key to scaling their business even further.

Chapter Sixteen
Efficient Organization

"Just so we are 100 percent clear, SK1, I'm holding your ass accountable if we can't find that damned fuse!"

The engineer had a reputation for holding people's feet to the fire, rather publicly too. This case was no exception. No one had any doubt that the supply petty officer's life was going to get miserable if he didn't find the fuse we needed.

Shortly after returning to San Diego from our eighteen-month overhaul in Washington, our boat went out to sea for training and exercises to get the crew ready for the next deployment. By this time, I was the division Leading Petty Officer (LPO), responsible for a twenty-man crew, only a few of whom had spent any length of time at sea before.

Every training underway like this was meant to do two things: train the crew and find out what would break. When you are thousands of miles from any land and submerged several hundred feet below the surface, that's not when you want to find out that you didn't train properly and your equipment wasn't adequate for the task at hand.

In this instance, we had run a simple Reactor SCRAM drill.[27] Everything was going smoothly since we were taking it easy on all the rookies out there. Didn't want to damage anything, or anyone, too early in their careers, after all.

---

27. The definition of SCRAM is in the glossary, but just think of it this way…if someone calls out "Scram!" the first inclination of someone would be to do just that…get the hell outta there!

One bank of rods had dropped as planned, the other remaining pulled for the time being, sort of like having only four pistons firing in a V-8 while the others remain lifeless. This was by design and nothing to worry about.

However, when it came time to pull the rods back out (the term we use for withdrawing the rods to achieve criticality in the reactor), a simple fuse blew in the circuitry, causing the rods to fall back to their initial starting point on the bottom of the reactor.

Shit happens, and we all know that. We train for that. This was nothing new.

Unfortunately, it wasn't going to be a routine drill anymore.

When the issue had been diagnosed and the cause determined, the supply team was called up and told exactly what part we needed.

In the Navy, as in most large organizations, everyone has a specialty. Cataloging and storing supplies and materials was no different. This was the job of the supply team, or "Store Keepers," SKs.

Their job was to store and inventory everything on the boat that was vital to the mission. Stowage in a submarine is quite different than anything you might have ever seen or heard of elsewhere.

Space is at a premium in a submarine, and with over 130 men crammed into a 300-foot tube, you can imagine how little room there was for mission-critical items, much less personal effects. Each crewmember was given a rack that acted as sleeping compartment and storage for their personal effects. The junior sailors got to "hot-rack," meaning that three sailors shared two racks, alternating their sleeping shifts.

Everything else that is needed to maintain the boat is stowed in lockers throughout the boat. With all the angles, pitches, and rolls a submarine can do, everything must be "stowed for sea," meaning in a locker or secured in some way so that it cannot fall out and break or injure someone underway.

These lockers look nothing like what you might think of in a typical locker room or even an industrial facility. Almost nothing is uniform, and there's no special row of lockers that you can quickly and easily peruse to find what you need. Instead, lockers come in every shape and size and are designed to simply fill the spaces where there isn't cabling, equipment, or walkways.

A locker can be found in almost every nook and cranny on a submarine—sometimes in the most obscure and ridiculous places that you can't even imagine getting your hand into, let alone equipment. On one occasion, in a locker hidden away behind electrical cables and steel frames, we found a coke and some books from a crewmember who had left the boat nearly two years prior. If we weren't ripping every locker out of the boat at that time, I have no doubt that coke would still be there today!

Given there are so many lockers on a submarine, and in such varying shapes and sizes, there needs to be a very concise way of cataloging and recording the contents of each locker. The first thing you need to do is number the lockers and have a clue where they are. Since some are hidden so well, conventional numbering simply won't work.

Instead, there's a system for numbering lockers, of all things! The system is straightforward once you understand it, and it makes perfect sense to a submariner.

A submarine is constructed of heavy-duty steel frames that are spaced a few feet apart for stability.[28] Each frame is also numbered so you have an idea of where on the boat you are, based on that number. For this reason, all lockers are numbered depending on the frames they are on or sitting between.

We also use port and starboard for the side of the boat you are on. Then, you have the level you are on (most submarines have three levels). This allows you

---

28. See http://www.marineinsight.com/naval-architecture/submarine-design-structure-of-a-submarine/ for some really cool information on why they do this, including what happens to a submarine if subjected to excessive external pressure.

to determine how fore or aft the locker is, on which side of the boat, and on which level it is located. This helps you narrow your search, but still only seasoned submariners know exactly where everything is located.

An example of a locker name might be ST-30-3-12, letting us know it is the twelfth locker on the third level, aft of frame 30 on the starboard side. That significantly narrows the search for the locker and, of course, its contents.

However, this was our supply petty officer's dilemma—the locker where the fuse was supposed to be located did not in fact have any fuses. Not only were they not in that locker, but they weren't anywhere else to be found or accounted for.

Without this fuse, there was no bringing the reactor online, and with several hundred miles between us and shore, the prospect of using the emergency propulsion motor to get us back home at three knots was not appealing. Not only would it take several days to traverse the seas, but to maintain battery power to run the propulsion motor, we'd need to continue running the diesel generator, which also had a finite amount of fuel.

To conserve fuel for the diesel, we would need to pursue our course surfaced, a very poor position for a submarine to be in. Submarines are meant to be submerged, not sitting on the surface being battered by waves back and forth. It wasn't uncommon to have twenty to thirty degree rolls in a moderate sea state, thus making every sailor sick to his stomach while the boat was bounced back and forth like a pendulum on the water.

To further aggravate the situation, a failure to get the reactor back up and running within a few hours meant shutting down everything and doing a cold startup at sea—a prospect not welcome in the least. It would require operating in conditions not typical of a submarine and meant even longer hours on watch.

The crew was getting restless and frustrated, and we began opening every locker not already accounted for. Tensions grew as the air conditioning and all non-vital loads were secured, thus causing a very hot environment where tempers were heated already. The temperature in the engine room could easily reach 130 degrees with the air conditioning running. Without A/C, the coolest temperatures in the engine room were nearing the triple-digit realm. This didn't bode well for our sensitive electronics, either.

To say it was a poor design to use only one very specific type of fuse that couldn't be substituted in any way was ridiculous. No alternative option could be found, and we dare not run the risk of "hotwiring" such a sensitive and critical component for a nuclear reactor.

The thought occurred to have the part flown in by helicopter and have one of us divers jump in the water to retrieve a package, and that option gained serious attention as the hours wore on. You could picture the entire engineering crew trying to figure this out, much like the scene in *Apollo 13* where Houston control was trying to find a way to preserve oxygen and eliminate harmful CO_2 for the astronauts. It was comical and infuriating at the same time.

Nearly eight hours later, just as the time was drawing near to shut down everything and limp on with barely enough power to keep the lights on (which in and of itself is a major hazard in a ship with no windows or sunlight), one crewmember found a fuse in the most hidden recess of the boat. Tucked away in a locker that wasn't even listed on the ship's registry, and which to the best of our knowledge had never been opened!

All hands were hard at work that day scouring the ship for anything we could find that might bring our power plant back to life and help us find our way back home. If it weren't for relentless persistence in the face of bleak conditions, we might very well have been pulled back home several hundred miles through open ocean, a complete embarrassment to the U.S. Navy and a stain on our operating record.

As luck would have it, we were able to install the fuse and get back up and running in short order, and no one was more relieved than SK1 Decker, who was just one cheek short of an ass!

Running a business efficiently and effectively is of course important as you scale up. Having a proper organizational structure and system in place is vital as well.

Time and again I find myself consulting with a client or in a business where I wonder how in the world anything gets done. Of no surprise, the main complaint of the business owner or executive is that they can't ever seem to get ahead. They haven't had any noticeable increase in revenue or profit for months, if not years, and their staff seems hell-bent on just getting by.

In *Beyond the Goal,* Eli Goldratt discusses proper organization for service-based businesses as it relates to bottlenecks within the company.[29] He points out that most organizations have a hard time increasing efficiency in their businesses from an administrative or sales process because they don't see the piles of paperwork sitting in an inbox as an issue.

Most people brush it off and conclude that "This is the way we've always done it," and "It has to be this way because of [X]!"

If you are finding yourself or your organization with this problem, there are three questions you must ask of yourself and your team:

1. What is the maximum output we can achieve per person working this way?

2. Is that output sufficient for us to scale and grow our business?

3. Assuming we want to scale and grow faster, how can we work through this process faster?[30]

---

29. You may not want to believe me, but in many cases the impediment to growth is seldom the people doing the work at the deck plate level. Generally, it is middle management or in some cases the C-suite because at those levels you're paid to think deep thoughts. This leads to analysis paralysis, and nothing happens. Take a chance or create a process for reducing risks, and you'll see your organization make more decisions faster with more results to show for it.
30. The very next question relating to the Optimize & Innovate theory is, "Okay, now that it's in place, how do we make it better?"

It may seem counterintuitive to some, but invariably when you start to explore answers to the third question, the first step is simply better organization.

Imagine if every time a fuse blew on our submarine, we had to start at locker #1 and work our way aft until we found the right fuse!

However, this is how many businesses work. They reinvent the wheel for nearly every process and thus lose massive amounts of efficiency. Many times, this is a result of an outdated process, or someone in a role who is considered the lynchpin for a specific procedure.

Take, for example, the organization I worked for where we didn't have a clearly defined qualification or development process for personnel. The last revision to the qualification process, which was required for state and national commissions, was in 1996!

In the years since then, the IT systems had changed, the testing requirements had changed, the equipment and technology people were getting qualifications to inspect had seen a complete revolution, and very few of the original training personnel were still with the company.

Thus, every time a new person came on board, the process of qualification needed to be reviewed and administered individually, and the individual receiving the training program was often confused and confounded as to how a Fortune 500 company could be so disorganized.

Further compounding the problem was that once you were initially qualified, there was no written process for these people to advance within the company. For that reason, some people were promoted to higher levels on a purely subjective basis, while other, more qualified individuals languished at the bottom because their managers didn't even know the process for promoting them!

Organization is simply the systematic compiling of information and data that allows someone who is completely unfamiliar with the system, process, or procedure to step in and find or figure out what they need. If you have people who are hoarding information like it is their baby, with no systematic organization of that information, then you are completely reliant on that person every time you need access to that data or information.

Even technology companies and startups who tell me how great their data is take several hours to explain why it is so great. In my opinion, the brilliance of information and data is in its simplicity. If it is simple to see, review, and understand, then it is achieving its goal.

Organization of information, processes, and procedures is necessary for the growth of your company.

I've talked at length about developing standard operating procedures, an absolute must for any organization. However, if those SOPs are hidden away in a notebook on some shelf in a storage unit, it does you and your business no good at all. SOPs must be organized in such a way that they are easy to find, consume, and implement.

Failure to organize your information, processes, and procedures could leave you with a blown fuse that can take down your business!

Chapter Seventeen
Whiskey Tango Foxtrot!

How to Communicate Like a Sailor[31]

Unkempt. Not the word you would normally use to describe a chief in the Navy, but Chief Holtz fit the description to a T most days.

A Navy chief is the equivalent of a middle manager in most organizations. They understand the business well and manage a large team of individuals in their division. They are also the role models for the junior sailors, the disciplinarians, the men and women who are expected to have their act together better than anyone else.

Many days, we'd have to remind him that his shirt was untucked partially and could barely focus on what he was saying because his hair appeared to have won the fight against the comb that morning. We also joked that his razor was two blades short of a full stack since stubble randomly appeared on his face in patches.

He wasn't a pretty face by any means, and half the time you'd wonder whether or not he knew where he was. We didn't bother Chief Holtz until at least the first cup of coffee was down. On a boat filled with sailors, testosterone could run high enough to want to pick a fight over the stupidest things sometimes, and Chief somehow managed to say something that would get your blood boiling within a few seconds if he hadn't woken up properly first.

---

31. Yes, we communicate differently. If you don't believe that, just take a glance at some of the glossary definitions. We could easily string together a full sentence of nothing but acronyms, and it would make sense!

Once he had his coffee and ran a hand through his hair a few times, he somehow switched on his brain and could start thinking. It was almost as if there were a fuel tank in him that was still completely empty when he woke that needed filling before he could function properly.

On only about two occasions each year, Chief Holtz would be the first at the Machinery Division workbench, before quarters, going through the task list and getting everything ready for the day.

"You boys ready to get started today?!?" he'd ask in an overly chipper voice.

"What's up, Chief? You get laid last night?" one of us would instinctively quip back.

"Damn right! Yesterday was my birthday. Now let's get shit cranking."

The other day of the year he'd be in such high spirits was his anniversary. I have to hand it to him, when he was on, he was on. Too bad it only happened twice a year for him.

"Fuck my life if that's ever me," Johnny D. whispered to me under his breath.

I nodded in agreement. Neither of us could imagine a life where sex twice a year was not only a reality, but accepted.

"There's always hookers!" Frankie chimed in from behind us. We all laughed and got back to work.

Chief Holtz either tended toward overly chaotic or extremely focused and overly critical. We either couldn't tell what was on his mind or couldn't get him to switch over to the other task that needed his attention.

One thing was for sure, though: no one knew more about submarine sailing and its history than Chief Holtz. The guy was an endless library of (some might say useless) information.³² But regardless of the relevance of his stories, he always managed to have an audience when he'd recall his "good ol' days." We assume they were the good old days because he wasn't responsible for a group of rowdy assholes like us back then.

"Back on the *Stonewall Jackson* when we ran this drill..." he began telling me as we were setting up for a routine reactor SCRAM drill, "...we actually got to shut down the whole thing. None of this playing pretend crap like we have to now."

Drills were where we honed our skills and learned more about the operations of the plant than during steady-state ops. We'd simulate something going wrong, then walk through the steps to recover.

My job this time was to monitor one valve that, if operated improperly during the drill, could result in massive damage to highly sensitive equipment that would force us into the shipyard for repairs. During our briefing, I was informed that under no circumstance was Valve B to be opened until pressure equalized across it through Valve A.

As the drill got underway without much fanfare, I walked around Maneuvering (where all the reactor and steam plant operations were managed) and saw the depth gauge. We were sitting at just a couple hundred feet deep when the drill began.

"Reactor SCRAM! Main steam isolation valves shut. Engineering watch supervisor, shift propulsion to the emergency propulsion motor," came the announcement over the 2MC speaker system.

All hands in the engine room immediately sprang to action, and steps were made to isolate the steam headers, shut down the turbines, and shift over to the electric motor that would keep us moving forward.

---

32. Yes, even me.

In a submarine, if you aren't moving forward, you're sinking. Regardless of the amount of air in the ballast tanks, a ship that heavy needs propulsion to maintain buoyancy while it is submerged. Once it is on the surface, the external pressure and weight of the water is no longer an issue, and the ship is safe to sit idle.

This was a routine drill that many of us had done several times before, but this time we had a few new faces manning certain stations. The isolation valve I was monitoring was shut properly, and everything seemed to be going along smoothly. The boat had begun an up-angle to bring us to periscope depth and then eventually to the surface. Having the reactor shut down and running on battery power or the diesel generator while submerged isn't ideal either.

You can feel the momentum of the boat to a certain extent while you're underwater. You don't have any windows or outside reference points to determine if you are moving forward or not, but you get used to the subtle sensations that tell you which direction you are going. In this case, it didn't feel like we were moving forward.

"Engineering watch supervisor, shift propulsion to the emergency motor!"

The order came over louder and a bit more intense. I made another round around Maneuvering and noticed that instead of moving toward the surface like we should have been, the depth gauge was going in the opposite direction.

"250 feet…300 feet…400 feet…500 feet…" It seemed to be picking up speed, and we could now feel the backward momentum on the ship.

"Engineering watch supervisor, EMERGENCY RESTORE THE ENGINE ROOM!"

This was a new order, one that I had never heard before, but I instinctively knew what it meant…

WE WERE SINKING AND NEEDED PROPULSION FAST!

"Barnes, open that valve right now!" Chief yelled at me on his way to his next station to bark orders.

"But pressure hasn't equalized yet, Chief."

"OPEN THE FUCKING VALVE! NOW!"

I began hammering away at the 18" handwheel, trying to get the valve to budge. With such an extreme pressure differential, it was damn near impossible to get the valve off its seat.

Frankie came over and gave me a hand. He had a lot more ass than me, so he was able to break it free.

The sound of steam rushing past the valve reminded me of the Sirens who caused Odysseus to cover his ears to avoid falling prey to their spells. It screamed incredibly loud, like a high-speed train going through a tunnel.

Soon the pressure equalized and we could open the valve the remainder of the way. Steam was now in the headers, and we were able to get one side of the propulsion plant back online in time to get the screw (propeller) moving again.

The ship slowed its backwards momentum and we all felt the shift in gravity as we began to move slowly toward the surface at first, and then picked up speed, escaping a drop below "crush depth"—the depth to which the engineers who designed the hull of the submarines said we should never approach.

I don't know how deep we went, but I do know there was a serious critique afterwards of what transpired during an otherwise routine drill, and more than one fresh pair of skivvies donned after that!

You would think, based on these stories I'm telling you, that all we did was fuck things up, right?

Fact of the matter is that our boat earned numerous commendations while we were underway, and our systems operated seamlessly for the most part (at least in our department).

What you may not have noticed was that these failures were a result of one common problem:

Poor Communication!

Poor (or in some cases a lack of) communication was at the heart of almost every major problem we had while I was in the Navy. Sometimes it was the result of some shithead (our term of endearment for someone who screws up) not paying attention or doing something in haste, and other times it was because we all assumed the other person knew what was going on.

In the situation I just described, what transpired was a failure of one individual to understand the order he was given, and another failure of the supervisor to not confirm that the order had been understood properly. This is precisely why the Navy has its own terminology and requires all ordered to be repeated back with an "aye" at the end to acknowledge and confirm proper receipt of the order. In this instance, that failed to happen, and we almost paid the ultimate price for this seemingly trivial error.

Going back to the procedures I told you to start writing, there is a reason we break the detail down to the gnat's ass before we split up complex tasks into seemingly braindead simple ones—someone is still going to mess them up.

You've also heard me refer to the various. communications systems throughout this book for good reason. Each one has a very distinct use and is designed specifically for that use. This is done to ensure that the right people are communicated with in the right way to achieve the desired result.

The Navy has its own vernacular, and submariners have a subculture to themselves. We get to use terms that would gross out a frat boy because we lived and breathed that life for so long and knew how to communicate with each other.

Similarly, the way you communicate with the people who work with you and for you will have a dramatic impact on how well your business fares long-term. Fail to communicate at all and you will likely lose good employees and have a high turnover rate.

Communicate badly and you just get bad results.

Communicate directly, remain transparent, and engage frequently, and you will likely begin to see improvements in your team and business.

My rule for communication is that more is better than less, and showing your hand too early will have fewer adverse side effects than you might think.

I know of many people, especially in larger organizations, who are afraid to give people good news too early in a process for fear that something might happen that prevents the good thing from coming to pass. There may be merit to this in some cases, but it really just tells me that you didn't properly set the expectations from the beginning.

A communications system is key to the growth of your organization. The flight attendants have the exact same script and procedure every single time you board a plane for good reason—failure to communicate the rules and dangers could result in chaos or worse in the event of an emergency.

In the Navy (while in port, anyway), we would have "Quarters on the Pier" every morning at 0800. This meant that every crewmember who was not currently on watch was required to attend a morning briefing with the management team. The captain wasn't always a part of this briefing because he had already briefed the department heads earlier, and they were conveying those messages to the rest of the crew.

Although obnoxious and tedious, what these meetings did was inform everyone of what was happening that day and what needed to happen and give everyone an update on the status of big-ticket items. This then led to meetings within the various departments to make sure everyone was on task to complete their projects, which gave us a chance to coordinate meetings with other divisions and departments.

We would then break out into our divisions and assign tasks to achieve our objectives, which were of course tied to the department's objectives, which in turn were tied to the ship's objectives.

Creating this top-down then bottom-up approach of communication was vital to the success of our missions and gave everyone a chance to voice concerns, comments, or objections, as well as to bring new information to light that may somehow impact whatever was happening that day.

Most companies fail at this type of communication on a colossal level. The only communication employees might get from on high is in the annual report to shareholders, and that's only if the employees read those, which very few do.

Other companies make a vain attempt at an electronic newsletter to inform their staff of what is going on. So impersonal and vague are these newsletters that after just a few issues, most employees stop reading them altogether as well.

Many companies are now conducting "town-hall" style events that relay big picture information from the CEO to the entire organization. While much better than nothing at all, these talks tend to be one-sided and lacking in transparency. They instead focus on just the big things that anyone could read about in the news—assuming they do that.

Bulletin boards, newsletters, email blasts, letters to shareholders, and town hall meetings are all fine, but they still miss one critical and key component:

They don't offer people at the lower rung of the ladder an opportunity to bring up any ideas or questions *in a safe environment.*

Even when the captain of a 120-crewmember submarine gets in front of the entire crew, he may ask if "anyone" has questions, but has little hope that the junior sailor will speak up with any concerns.

Instead, he leaves that to his middle managers and front-line supervisors. Those are the people who are key to bringing up issues "from the deck plate" to the boardroom because they directly touch the equipment and operate the machinery. However, without any forum for this to happen in a safe environment, it just doesn't happen at all. If you can remember when you first started in your career how intimidating it might have been to chat with the CEO of a Fortune 500 company, you might be able to comprehend the importance of creating this "safe" approach to bottom-up communication.

Even in our new-age, open-concept, Millennial-infused organizations, one of two things will happen if no safe environment is provided for this type of communication:

The most junior person will feel entitled to speak his mind, having no clue about the context of an issue, or be completely oblivious to the ramifications of his/her suggestions, and upon making them at an inopportune time find that others are only half-interested in their opinion and appear condescending in their response…OR

No communication will occur at all, and the executive will be left with a warm fuzzy feeling that he has all the information he needs to make an informed decision, however inaccurate that assessment may be. Thus, decisions are made from the boardroom without accurate information, those at the lower levels will feel that decisions are made absent any "real world" experience, and the executive will lose the respect of the people he relies upon to carry out the mission of the business.

In either case, the long term result is that communication is stymied in the organization, and the C-suite executives are left trying to make all of the important decisions without accurate information. This leaves them wondering why initiatives are not fully embraced when rolled out, and frustrated at the apparent lack of motivation by the troops to carry out the mission.

Many times, executives arrive at the conclusion that they need to "motivate" their employees in some fashion and then spend an inordinate amount of time and money on trying to get people on board. In fact, the solution is simple, though not always easy.

Instituting a process for clear and precise communication in both directions, along with a safe environment for junior personnel to voice their opinions, will help with the buy-in process for any decisions made. Further, it will potentially mitigate making rash decisions absent deck-plate-level information that could prove useful for making such a decision.

The fact is that the only way to avoid a crisis in your business is to ensure that everyone clearly understands what is expected of them on a regular basis and that they know *why* these expectations are set. People are much more willing to do what they need to do when they understand why they are doing it. I was trained to obey orders in the Navy, but I was also trained to question those orders if they appeared to conflict with proper operations and practices.

So, although I was told to absolutely, positively, under no circumstances allow that valve to be turned without first ensuring the prerequisites were met, when I heard the order to emergency restore the engine room, and the subsequent order from my chief, I had all the reason I needed to violate the original dictum and comply.

Having a process for communication in your business may not save your life someday, but it will hopefully keep your business afloat and prevent you from sinking in your own ship!

Chapter Eighteen
Optimize, Innovate, Transform

Ultimately, there are only two ways to grow your business: get more customers or increase the value of every existing customer you have. Many people break it down a little bit more by saying you can:

Increase the number of customers you acquire.

Increase the number of purchases made by each customer.

Increase the average transaction size of each customer.

In essence, two and three are really just increasing the average value of each customer, also referred to as the customer lifetime value (CLV).[33]

I've talked about the systems you need to increase the customer's value throughout this book by using your operational system to spur on repeat business and increase transaction size by offering value far in excess of what your customer pays or expects.

Now I want to talk about growing your company by putting all of these systems together into one system that so many people simply give lip service to: **Innovation.**

Innovation, as a system, is a core component of every business's growth trajectory, though in many cases it is simply an afterthought, or considered

---

[33]. I speak at length about how you can use these three strategies to grow your business in another book, *The Small Business Success Blueprint,* which is provided in the bonus section online at www.AngelNetwork.com/bonus.

beyond the reach of their business. However, innovation doesn't need to be a complex, ambiguous, and ethereal process that is hard to understand.

After having sat through hundreds of discussions with entrepreneurs, executives, and multimillion-dollar businesses, I can tell you that what passes as innovation in many people's minds would hardly be worth the ink on this page. The reason is because they keep thinking that to be innovative, they must be the next Steve Jobs, Mark Zuckerberg, or Larry Page. They must create the next Google, Tesla, self-driving car, or unmanned spacecraft.

What they don't realize is that being innovative doesn't require a propensity for being an inventor like Thomas Edison, so they are always looking for the most creative solution to problems that don't exist, instead of focusing on how to make their existing business better.

Since I'm not writing this book for the dreamer entrepreneur who wants to build the next Facebook, Snapchat, or Tesla, we will focus instead on realistic, useful, and pragmatic innovation to grow your business.

To do this, we must first discuss why you need an innovation system to begin with. I look at this through the lens of your customers, and you should too. Never think about innovating simply to make something new and shiny, but rather to provide even more value to your customers. Or, to think differently about it, *"How can you improve your products, services, or operations in such a way that your customers never leave you for an alternative solution?"*

Disney, for example, hasn't created a new "category" or technology for its theme parks, but has rather innovated on the idea and experience of theme parks to remain the preeminent leader in that space. They do this by first understanding where they add value and where they fit in the value stream.

As I mentioned earlier, everything you do should focus on adding value to a customer using your "Unique Value Proposition"—the one thing that no other competitor can replicate that your customers love about doing business with you.

Once you know your unique value proposition, you must turn that into a "value statement" that conveys your unique value proposition to your customer in a way that they can see and grasp what it is that you can do for them.

For my consulting clients, I help them understand that I can double their business by helping them optimize, innovate, and transform their business processes and procedures utilizing the same principles as U.S. Navy Submarine.[34]

This is derived from my Unique Value Proposition, or Selling Proposition, as the only consulting company that uses the principles of a U.S. submarine to transform and grow service-based businesses.

You will need to do the same thing in your business, and that starts first by identifying the *gap* that you fill in your customers' lives. The gap is simply identifying the before state and future state of your customer and how you help them get from the before state to the future state.

This is known as the value stream. The value stream, or value chain as many refer to it, is the entire process that goes from the beginning of where you first start the customer identification and engagement process all the way through until you have solved their problem, with every little step in between.

One thing you will want to understand is that there are entire value chains for the pipeline of activities required to provide the end customer with the final product or service, and then there are value chains for each individual business, department, and division within that value chain that should be broken out.

---

34. Big claim, yes, and maybe not believable for some people, but the truth is that if I can't do that, then I didn't do my due diligence before I took the client on. You need to make sure your value proposition is designed for your ideal customer.

When we do this, we employ "Lean Principles" originally pioneered by Toyota in the 1960s to improve organizational efficiency, which allowed them to revolutionize not only the auto industry, but every manufacturing industry in the world. These same principles can (and should) be applied to every aspect of your business to help you do the first part of the innovation system: **Optimize!**

By optimizing various business processes, you can accomplish two things:

You identify the various areas within your business that can be improved or eliminated, thus eradicating all those fires you keep putting out, AND

You free up time and resources to focus on how you can now add more value to your customers and grow the business!

In the figure on the next page is a simplified example of a value stream for a reinsurance company I worked with. If you think it is overly simplified, it is, but that is for a very good reason—these are the steps that must be taken to add value to the customer.

Anything that is put in place in this value chain must achieve the same goal: increase the value to the customer.

If it doesn't increase value, then it doesn't need to be in there, or it needs to be dramatically scaled down so that it doesn't create wasted time, effort, money, or other resources.

This leads to the second phase of OIT: **Innovate!**

As I mentioned earlier, innovation isn't simply about creating the next out-of-this-world invention; it can mean reimagining your entire business to refocus your energy on your customer.

To achieve this, you must again look at all the steps in your value chain, and after optimizing each step to the best of your ability, figure out which steps you can reimagine to add more value.

I will use an example to help you understand this.

Let's say you are a service company that sends technicians into the field to perform repair work for your customers and most of your customers are small businesses. When you send your service technician out, they likely have a work order of some sort that lays out basic information about the customer for the tech, as well as some information about the job.

However, you find that your technician spends more time explaining to the customer what the problem is than he spends fixing the problem, which of course adds to your expenses and reduces your margins.

Instead, let's gear the technician with an iPad and an app that he hands to the customer upon arrival. The app is preloaded with the customer's contact info but ensures that we have a good mailing and email address so we can follow up later.

Then the app goes on to explain what the likely cause of the problem they are experiencing is. It has a video demonstration of what the technician is doing, as well as how the problem might have begun in the first place.

Example of a Value Chain for a Reinsurance Insurance Company

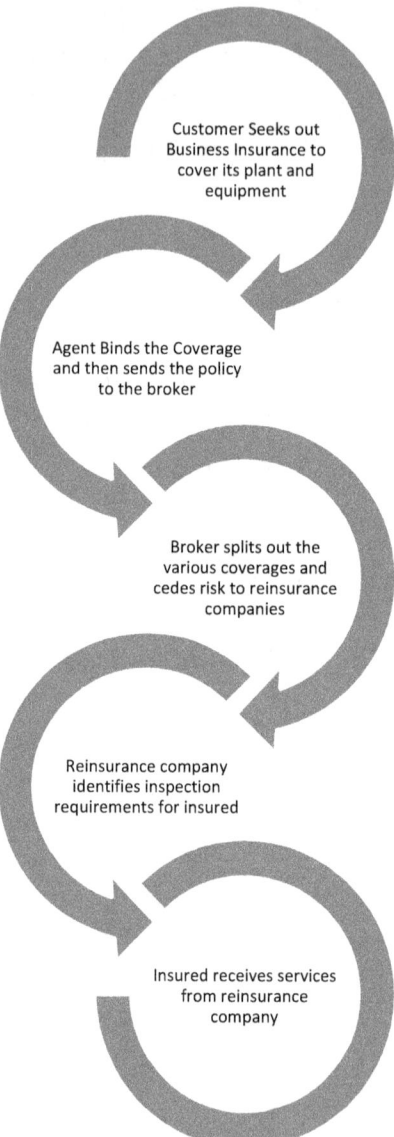

It engages the customer and has a short quiz at the end to find out more about their business. Once that is done, the customer is immediately directed to another video, in this case a sales video that is based 100 percent on their answers to the quiz and the initial reason for the visit.

Let's further pretend the issue was a slow computer network that was caused by a virus that no one was aware of having been downloaded in an email.

This sales video explains that for an additional $39 per month, the service technician can come out on a monthly basis, verify that everything is working properly and no new viruses have been added to the network, and he can perform a quick diagnosis of their entire system.

It can then ask them if they'd like continuous monitoring of their system to prevent future attacks that their firewall didn't stop, and further offer them insurance in the event anything goes wrong and they need to replace or repair the network again.

By this time, the technician has likely finished the job, come back to the customer, explained what he did, and reiterated the value of these additional services. The customer is now pleased that the problem has been fixed, there is a solution in place to prevent future problems – they won't need to stress about down time, stolen data, or lost business ever again, and if anything does happen, they are 100 percent covered!

This whole process is incredibly innovative for most businesses and allows a few things to happen that are not occurring at all:

The technician's time is spent doing what is considered his *zone of genius*—fixing the problem and not being a salesperson.

The customer is being informed of what happened and how to prevent it again (this is called education-based marketing).

You are gathering further insights into your customer's business that you can leverage for immediate and future sales and services.

The customer, who just purchased from you in a time of need, has been educated on more products and services you have that they can purchase on the spot without your non-salesperson technician fumbling it up.

Your customer is now paying you an ongoing fee (continuity) for services that will require very little if any additional man-hours, thus increasing your profit margins.

No one else is doing anything like this, and as a result your customer is locked into your business for as long as you continue to provide exemplary service!

Again, the important thing to understand when you begin mapping out your value chain is the need to look at the whole flow from the initial request all the way through to the final completion and delivery to the customer, as well as the value chain for each business unit so you can streamline, optimize, innovate, and transform those processes to add even more value to your customer.

The goal isn't simply to improve operational efficiency, which is the ultimate goal of most novice lean practitioners, but instead to find new ways to add value to your customer while improving your internal processes at the same time. This increases the value to your bottom line, as well as your value in the marketplace. It enhances your value proposition and continues to answer the question for your customers:

"Why should I do business with you, over and above any other option available to me, including doing nothing?"

When you innovate processes in your value chain with an eye on customer retention and enhancing the customer's lifetime value, you can't help but win!

This then brings us to the final opportunity within your operational system: *Transform Your Business!*

Using the previous example, you have gone from a simple service provider company for a single service to a complete front-to-end solution for anything related to their network and infrastructure.

You can transform everything about your business by now focusing on all the areas of your customer's business that you can improve. You begin to open up opportunities where none existed before, because now you have processes in place that no competitor has, and you have a system to ensure you will be enhancing that value on a regular basis.

With this new operational system in place, you can:

- Create partnerships with similar but noncompeting businesses to add complementary services as part of a service package (such as insurance as part of your service-delivery).

- Create more in-depth marketing and customer retention road maps that enhance and deliver value long after you've left, thus bringing customers back again and again.

- Hire and train more experienced and qualified staff to perform higher level services and increase the value of every visit.

This transforms you from an "only when I'm in dire straits and need someone right now" type of business to one that is constantly at the forefront of what your customers need.

As an example, I had a water leak in my house one time that resulted in the walls, floors, insulation, and even water heater itself being ruined. The plumber came in, cut out the leaking pipe, replaced the pipe and water heater, and left.

He could have:

- Provided floor drying services and mold testing as an ongoing service to ensure we didn't have a mold issue.

- Partnered with an HVAC company to replace the insulation on the ducting because it was damp and nasty.

- Partnered with a carpet company to replace our carpet and earn a referral fee.

- Suggested a leak detection or monitoring service that his company offered as a way to get ongoing revenue.

- At the very least, added my information to a Customer Relationship Management (CRM) system to provide ongoing offers and deals to keep me as a customer.

As it stands, that was nearly two years ago and I haven't heard from his company since. All I have is a silly magnet that holds the kids' artwork up on the fridge as a reminder of how damn expensive it was for him to cut a hole in my furnace room ceiling that persists to this day.

Chapter Nineteen
The Key Ingredient

There I was, standing in the engineer's stateroom at modified parade rest—fists clenched behind my back, jaw set, and staring straight ahead—receiving the worst tongue lashing I'd ever received. The stream of obscenities spewing out of the mouth of our engineer was enough to make the devil blush.

"Un-fucking believable, Barnes! How could you of all people let this shit happen? If it wasn't for your fucking division our department would have passed this ORSE with flying colors! Instead, I have to go back to squadron with my dick in my hand and explain why we couldn't manage to follow a fucking procedure that *you fucking wrote! EXPLAIN YOURSELF!*"

It was all I could do to keep from yelling right back at the engineer, dubbed the "Prince of Darkness" on our boat.

My first inclination was to point fingers and place blame on the idiot who screwed up, but I knew that wouldn't get me very far. I realized that the only thing I could do was own up to my own shortcomings in hopes of shutting down the ass-chewing as quickly as I could.

"No excuse, sir. It was my fault for not correcting the procedures to begin with, not anyone else's. It will be corrected immediately."

"Well it fucking better! Not that it's going to make one goddam bit of difference. You already fucked me and everybody else on this one. Get the fuck out of here, and I expect a corrected procedure in my hands before chow!"

"Aye, sir," I replied, and then made a quick about-face and headed back to the engine room.

"*Fucking Bear Claw,*" I muttered under my breath as I made my way back to the engine room, ego sorely bruised and heart rate and blood pressure at unhealthy levels.

The Occupational Reactor Safeguard Examination, commonly referred to as ORSE, is an annual review of any Naval vessel operating a nuclear reactor. The crew trains religiously for this exam, and we're expected to be on point in every capacity throughout the entire process.

The exam consists of three full days (and nights) of record reviews, administrative reviews, practical exams, drills, and a fine-tooth groom of everything imaginable in the engineering department. Failing to pass ORSE could result in the ship being docked pierside, the engineer and captain being stripped of their command, and the ship being unable to support the missions of the fleet.

To say that it is an important process would be an understatement.

However, we just screwed up, royally, and all I could think of was how much I wanted to beat the living shit out of the guy who fucked it up for us: Bobby "Bear Claw" Baker.

Baker was the product of a grossly undermanned naval force and the result of low expectations. Book smart, common sense inept, and socially retarded, every one of us wondered how he had managed to make it to the fleet as a nuc. It truly baffled the mind.

Baker was one of those guys whom we had to keep in the bilge or ass end of the boat to hide him from everything and everyone who was important. Somehow, everything we let him work on turned to shit, and the rest of us ended up picking up the slack.

Baker was a world class shit bag and buddy-fucker. He'd consistently show up late to his watch, need to be relieved early so he wouldn't shit his pants (there's no head in the engine room), and he always looked like he just got steamrolled by a shit tanker. His overweight, glossy-eyed, deer-in-the-headlights demeanor let everyone around him know that he had no desire to be a star performer.

On one occasion while we were still in port, when the oncoming duty section was briefing for a rather important evolution, Baker strolled in ten minutes late to the briefing, looking like he'd just rolled out of his bunk and put on a poopy-suit (coveralls) that hadn't been washed in a month. His hair was pointing in every direction, and his belt buckle was screaming for mercy—flipped upside down from his protruding gut.

In one hand he carried a box from the local grocery store that he had apparently needed to stop at on his way to work. In the other hand he had a pastry, half eaten, with crumbs and glaze still covering his face like a toddler after eating toast with jam.

"Whatcha got there Baker? You bring donuts for all of us for showing up late?"[35] ET1 Grover asked.

In the Navy, showing up late is only excusable by a couple of things, and eating donuts you stopped to get isn't one. The only saving grace he might have had was if he had bought them for everyone so we would all forget what a shit bag he was…for a minute.

"Nope," came his full-mouthed reply, crumbs flying out as he spoke. "Just a few bear claws for my breakfast."

"Are you fucking kidding me?" hollered Grover.

"You brought a whole fucking box of bear claws for yourself?!? And you showed up late? Guess who's getting the first and last watch today…Bear Claw!" We all erupted in laughter, because that nickname fit like a glove.

---

35. That's standard practice—you show up late, you bring food for the rest of us. Gives the shit bags incentive to show up for work. Underway, these guys suffer serious torment if they show up for their watch or a briefing late.

Baker wouldn't have a chance to finish his beloved bear claws prior to going on watch that day, and he ended up going back on watch at midnight that night to finish the rotation—a fair punishment for showing up late.

That was Baker. That was the guy whom the ORSE team decided to hone in on for various evolutions that needed to be performed as part of the machinery division's assessment.

When we saw the list of evolutions that were chosen, and who would be running them, we all immediately threw our hands up in the air and had the collective thought of, "Well…we're fucked!"

Baker had been chosen to start up the reverse osmosis unit, a rather simple evolution of turning a few valves and bringing seawater into the unit that would then be distilled into fresh water for the plant and potable water.

Our ship had the first ever installation of this type of reverse osmosis unit. It was designed to support the crew and plants with all the freshwater we would need without using steam like our previous distilling system had.

As a result of being the first to install and use the new unit, we were also tasked with coming up with the procedure required to start up and operate the unit properly. This meant sequencing every electrical and mechanical operation that needed to happen to go from a complete standstill and isolated status to fully functioning and bringing water down the header as quickly as possible without complication.

It took several months of tweaking the procedure while our boat was put back together in the shipyard, but eventually we had everything written down, tested, and approved. The only problem was that we were testing everything pierside without the actual operational parameters available.

When we headed to sea after our shipyard availability, we once again began testing the systems and verifying that our procedures worked properly. Although most steps held up well, the change in sea pressure and salinity dictated how we operated various valves and other components to get the unit humming along as needed.

Some of these changes we recorded and made a standing memo, others we had incorporated into the operating procedures. The challenge was one of time and resources. We all had competing priorities, and we all *knew* how to run the RO unit. However, in naval terms, if something isn't written down in a procedure, it doesn't exist.

I learned that lesson the hard way (again) when Baker began the evolution with me as his oversight. We were both being graded by the lieutenant from the ORSE team as we walked through the evolution. Baker was tasked with starting the unit, I was tasked with grading Baker, and the Lt. was tasked with grading us both.[36]

The evolution progressed with several issues found with the procedure and the operator, as I had anticipated. I took several notes on Baker's ineptitude as he fumbled through the procedure: at times incorrectly calling out for valves to be opened when it wasn't time, calling the Engine Room Supervisor (ERS) to assist, and the lower level watch calling out our (supposedly) more senior upper level watch who was in charge of the operation.

After the evolution persisting for what felt like an eternity with the Lt. staring over my shoulder and writing notes on his clipboard, never once uttering a sound, we finished. From there it was time to debrief Baker on the evolution, again with the lieutenant's oversight. I explained Baker's mistakes to him as we would in a normal coaching and development situation, and we ended the evolution as best we could.

---

36. In business, you want redundancies for everything that is important to the success of your company. In nuclear power, you want the same, plus redundancies on how you train and qualify people. We qualify the qualifiers who then examine the examiners.

All of these memories flashed through my mind as I made my way aft to rip Baker a new asshole when it finally dawned on me the error of my ways. Baker wasn't to blame. Shit bag that he was, he still wasn't to blame.

"Baker," I called to him in the engine room by our machinery bench, "What the fuck happened back there during the RO evolution? What went wrong?" I asked.

"Uh…" Typical deer in the headlights response I was accustomed to from him.

"Never mind. I'll just tell you. What went wrong is that you didn't follow procedure, and the evolution was a complete failure. Why didn't you follow procedure?"

"Because…" he started in.

"Because I let you down," I cut him off.

He stopped, goofy mouth hanging open in stunned silence as he stared at me through his Coke-bottle lenses waiting for me to continue.

"I let you down Baker, because we trained you how to start up the RO unit the right way, and you actually did what you were trained to do, surprisingly. You even made your best effort to explain to the Lt. and me why you were deviating from the procedure to do what we trained you to do.

"Unfortunately, I failed because you shouldn't have had to do that. As the LPO (Leading Petty Officer) and AQAO (Assistant Quality Assurance Officer), it's my job to make sure that our operating procedures are correct and on point. We knew there were issues with the procedure, and I let you and everyone else down by not making sure they were properly fixed prior to our deployment.

"For that, I apologize."

Again, stunned silence. Baker had become accustomed to the typical ass-chewing that accompanies a fuck up of this magnitude and didn't know how to respond to my leniency in this matter.

"However, since you now understand that we have something that needs to be corrected, I'm going to ask you to correct the procedure with my review, and verify it works…today. Can you do that?"

Baker's demeanor shifted from the downtrodden toddler who was being punished to a man with a purpose. His head lifted, eyes brightened, and shoulders pulled back, he replied, "With pleasure," and got to work.[37]

What I came to realize after that instance was not that Baker was blameless in all situations, but that he and so many others truly needed direction, guidance, support, and a full understanding of why they were being asked to do something.

Months earlier, when I was tasked with getting a procedure finalized for the RO unit, I had brushed it off as something insignificant and "beneath me." I felt that I was overqualified for something so silly, and that any fool with half a mechanical brain could get the damn thing running.

Later, when I realized that the procedure was flawed, I had the same response. *We know what we're doing, so who cares?*

It wasn't until the engineer chewed me up one side and down another that the full importance of my actions began to sink in. It wasn't about the ORSE exam. We still passed and our boat earned the coveted Battle "E" Award for that deployment.

---

37. I wish I could say I changed his life around, but after I left the boat I heard he went back to his same lackadaisical manners and did some really stupid stuff, got caught, then lied about it. Long and short, you can't motivate the unmotivated and you can't always fix the broken, but it doesn't mean you don't try to lift up those around you.

What I finally understood was that the procedure was a vital component to something much bigger. The reverse osmosis units made drinking water out of seawater, and it was the only piece of equipment on board that could tackle that feat.

Potable water is consumed in the thousands of gallons per day by the crew for everything from showering, eating, doing laundry, and cooking to highly critical tasks such as cooling the electrical components that operate the ship, and if necessary, being further distilled for use in the reactor itself.

Although I knew I could run the RO unit blindfolded in my sleep, it was the procedure that would permit everyone else to operate the unit when I or another senior person wasn't around. We were there from the outset, so we knew how to use the equipment, but what about the rest of the fleet that was about to get this same equipment?

There are several things that are mission critical for a submarine. Water is definitely one of them. No water, no mission.

My actions, though seemingly innocent to me at the time, could have severely hampered the ability of our submarine force to properly carry out and execute on our missions. I have no doubt that someone else would have (or may have already) figured out our errors and fixed them properly. However, how many man-hours would have been wasted in this pursuit?

The fact is that there is no way to properly run any organization, whether it be a nuclear powered submarine, a Fortune 500 Company, or a nonprofit, without clearly defined and proven standard operating procedures (SOPs). These SOPs are what allow managers and leaders of an organization to avoid putting out fires and instead focus on the continued growth of the organization.

Without SOPs to govern how you do most of what you do, you will be continuously plagued with unending questions, problems, and challenges that your staff face.

Implement SOPs, then focus on holding people accountable to follow them, and your life as a leader will vastly improve!

Chapter Twenty
Owning Your Role

"Barnes, you want to run the show?" Senior Chief was eyeballing me on the mess decks, his glare intent, wondering how I'd respond.

"Say again, Senior Chief,"[38] I replied, curious what he was getting at.

"You want to sit in the chair for the drills today?"

Drills were never-ending while we were underway. If we weren't cleaning, sitting through training, eating, or on mission, we were running drills. It was the only way to prepare for what could go wrong. Anything from a torpedo being fired at us to a steam line rupture in the engine room—we trained on it regularly. Today, I knew we were going to run a drill that involved shutting down the reactor and bringing it back online in the middle of the ocean, a few hundred feet below the surface.

"Sure," I shot back, jumped up, and headed to Maneuvering in the engine room.

I was working on my Engineering Watch Supervisor qualifications, the highest qualification I could achieve at my rank. It meant running the engine room and all staff while we were underway and ensuring everything ran smoothly.

I entered Maneuvering to quizzical glances from the crew, wondering why I was back there after just being relieved for my watch.

---

38. Say again = please repeat yourself? Typical response from a senior official: "Unfuck yourself and open your ears!"

"The EDMC wants me to sit in the chair for the drills coming up," I commented to help them get why I was there.

"We have Ensign Clark sitting in the chair for the under instruction[39] this time around, Barnes. Sorry," the Engineering Officer of the Watch (EOOW) told me.

"How about you sit Reactor Operator instead?" he continued.

Shit. I hadn't studied everything I needed to know for the RO spot, and it wasn't part of my qualification process. But I also knew that, as a mechanic, it was very unlikely I'd ever get another chance to sit as the reactor operator again.

"Sure, sir. Would love to," came my reply.

One of my buddies, Frankie, laughed and thought the whole idea was crazy. This guy, though bat-shit crazy at times, knew more about the process of running a reactor than anyone else I'd met in his position and probably would have challenged Admiral Rickover on how to run a reactor if he'd had the chance!

However, Frankie agreed and hopped up to let me sit down in his chair. The reactor operator's spot is in the middle of the three control panels in Maneuvering, directly in front of the EOOW for maximum visibility. The controls were antiquated, and even the digital readouts are laughable compared to today's digital technology.

However, there I sat, soaking it up and controlling the pumps and control rods to manipulate reactor power. We reviewed procedures for some possible drill scenarios, and at about the time I was going through one of the manuals, the engineer and other drill coordinators entered.

---

39 An "under instruction" or UI is a person who is literally under the instruction of a fully qualified person. In other words, on the job training.

It was game time, and I was stoked!

Shortly thereafter, the drill commenced and the reactor scrammed without any warning at all.

"Reactor SCRAM, commencing SCRAM procedures," I called out to the EOOW.

We completed our immediate actions, which are required to be 100 percent committed to memory.[40] There's no time when dealing with forces this great to pull out manuals and review procedures.

We got the main steam valves shut and confirmed all operating parameters were within normal limits, verifying that the plant was in a stable condition, and pulled out the manuals to completely verify we had followed all procedures correctly.

While all of this was going on, I kept wanting to blurt out to the EOOW what the next steps should be from his perspective, but he was in training too, and that might be overstepping too much.

As it stood, my mind raced, thinking of the next actions, hoping my division and crew in the engine room were doing their actions correctly. At times, my mind drifted to what was happening in the engine room, and I forgot to keep an eye on my panel.

"BARNES!"

The EOOW had been talking, but I assumed it was to someone else. Having not ever sat in the chair before, I forgot my title was "Reactor Operator" and that I was supposed to respond accordingly.

---

40. There's a procedure for everything, but you do things often enough and you remember them in the event there's an emergency. Better to know how to steer the car clear of danger than to try to pull out the manual when you're in the middle of an emergency.

"Yes sir? Preparing to pull rods," I snapped back into action, reviewing the procedure with Frankie and making sure I was on target.

I wasn't accustomed to being the person being told what to do anymore. I oversaw my division and personnel in the engine room, not to mention that I was damn good at what I did, so being told what to do next and reminded of a procedure I wasn't completely prepared for caught me off guard.

As we began recovering the plant and pulling the rods, I realized that the handle I was twisting wasn't responding as I'd hoped.

"Quit limp-wristing[41] it, Barnes, and get those rods out!" blurted the engineer.

He was right, all indications were that I was not keeping pace with where we needed to be to start bringing steam back down the header and getting propulsion back. In my line of work, I regularly turned thirteen-inch solid steel handwheels that required more ass than one person could put into them, so the thought of "muscling" a tiny black plastic handle on a control board seemed like a silly idea.

However, there I was falling behind on my duties and not getting us back up to speed as was required of me.

I shimmed the rods out further and faster to get back on track, starting to notice the lagging effect of our temperature and pressure sensors on my actions.

"Slow down, turbo!" Frankie chimed in, making sure I didn't overshoot my mark.

Funny thing—controlling nuclear fission reactions is a somewhat delicate task! Not something a knuckle-dragging mechanic like myself was accustomed to.

---

41. As in, "Stop being a pussy and put some muscle into it!"

All rods in their correct position and steam being brought down the header to restore the engine room, I completed my logs and documented the actions I'd taken.

"Respectfully request to be relieved, sir?" I asked the EOOW.

"With pleasure, Barnes."

Knowing our true purpose is difficult, nigh impossible at times. However, it's gaining this understanding that helps us to propel forward and truly make an impact.

Part of understanding your purpose comes down to understanding what you are not just good at, but great at. Being good gets you a pat on the back.

Being great gains you the respect and admiration of those around you, and the various benefits that accompany such greatness. Jim Collins's book *Good to Great* outlines how businesses make this leap, and it is important to understand this concept.

The first thing to realize is that good is the enemy of great. Being *good enough* hampers you from achieving greatness. However, most people suffice with simply being good at something.

It's hard to say how many times I've learned this all too important lesson in life. Every time I got to be good at something, people became satisfied with my work or contribution and didn't expect much more. In other words, I was average.

In the Navy, being a "3.0 Sailor" is considered being average. It means you've done everything expected of you, but that is about all. Most people I know aren't okay with being "3.0" (said "three point oh"). On a five-point scale, leaders strive for 5.0, and getting an average score is akin to a kick in the nuts.

However, that's where most people sit, if they warrant recognition at all.

The key ingredient to growing your business by implementing the various systems, processes, and procedures I've outlined in this book comes right down to this concept.

You can't achieve exceptional growth by running a 3.0 business or team.[42]

The true key to implementing all of this is understanding what I refer to as your **Zone of Genius** (ZOG), which I mentioned in a previous chapter. But beyond that, it's relinquishing everything else that isn't in your ZOG to others who have that skillset.

The key ingredient in all of this is having a team that complements every aspect of what you are trying to achieve. Too many times I find people who try to take on everything by themselves and end up failing, blaming the world for their shortcomings. They are operating at 3.0 because they chose to operate outside of their zone of genius.

Jim Rohn's mentor, Earl Shoaff, asked Jim why he hadn't succeeded yet in obtaining his goals. Rohn gave an account of all the reasons he hadn't achieved his goals yet—blaming society, time, upbringing, and his lack of resources, among others. When Shoaff heard Jim's full account, he replied:

"Well son, that's a damn fine list of reasons, but there's only one problem. **You ain't on it!**"

The very real problem that most businesses have when trying to implement operational systems, processes, and procedures is that the people at the helm stand in the way of their own success. They are unwilling to look in the mirror and tell the person staring back at them to get out of the way and let people help them.

They insist on developing these processes in a closed boardroom with their C-suite executives there by their side applauding their efforts, but they never look

---

42. In Navy terms, a 3.0 sailor is average, or maybe just above average by a gnat's ass. Every self-motivated sailor looks to be a 5.0 on the five-point scale.

beyond those four walls to identify the real problems. The business owner or executive who tries to singlehandedly reengineer his business is doomed from the outset. And upon failing or falling short of his goals, he blames the employees, the customers, the computers, or whatever he can rather than acknowledging that it was the approach that failed, not those other things.

As an example, a company I worked for invested over $10 million in a new enterprise resource planning (ERP) and customer relationship management (CRM) tool. The program was developed by a contracted company with little understanding of the day-to-day operations of the people who would be using it, and then it was reviewed and tested by others in the company without a full understanding of the processes in the field either.

As a result, when the program was rolled out, nearly 30 percent of the staff quit within two years, and even a decade later there were still people complaining about the program and flaws in the system. If after a couple years the Navy couldn't get a certain style of valve to work properly, they would have looked for alternatives rather than spending another eight years forcing people to use a defective piece of equipment.

However, that is the issue I find time and again with most businesses—the bureaucracy and egotism cloud the judgment and ability of the executives and managers to implement lasting and beneficial change. People are unwilling to admit to making a mistake they feel would hurt their image but are more than willing to further an agenda that hurts the company.

Of course there is a cure for this, and it goes right back to the story I relayed in the beginning of this chapter. The solution can be either as easy or as hard as you'd like to make it. I will attempt to outline a simple solution for implementing these dramatic changes to your organization to achieve a truly customer-centric operational model.

It All Comes Down to Money

You hear time and again that a business's sole purpose is to acquire and keep customers for the purposes of turning a profit. I like to add to that and say that your job as a business owner is to make your customers' lives better at a profit.

If that's the case, then anything you do in your business should be to make your customers' lives better, right? This should in turn result in more value for them and more money for you.

Now the important thing to understand is that unless you are the only person in your business and always plan to be solo, you likely aren't the main or only person engaging with your customers. Even in a solo-operator business, you're still likely not the best person to implement what I've laid out in this book.

So, if you aren't the person engaging with your customers daily, then how do you lead the change that impacts your customers for the better?

You start by building a team that does engage the customer up and down the value chain. If you have different types of customers (consumers, agents, brokers, etc.), then you want the people who help each of these customer segments to work hand in hand with you and your implementation team.

You can't make decisions in isolation or separated from your customers by layers of bureaucracy. But you also can't assume that everyone who works with your customers is best suited to help you build an operational system.

You must begin by identifying your star players who are willing, enthusiastic, and motivated to make changes to help provide a superior customer experience. To find the right people and build the right team, you can do several things:

- Hold an idea contest.

Ask everyone in your organization to submit ideas on how to improve the business, then have these ideas discussed openly. The people whom you see submitting the most ideas and engaging regularly with others are likely the people who want to implement positive changes.[43]

- Pull from a pool of your rising stars.

    Most large companies have some sort of talent management or career development process that identifies people at all levels who are exceedingly bright and ambitious. Reach out to them and ask them for their ideas on how to make the business better.

- Pull a fast one!

    On NBC's *The Partner* with Marcus Lemonis, Marcus has three fake pitches given to his contestants to find out what their reactions will be. It's only later on that he says they were all a sham aimed at getting them to voice their opinion and not being afraid to speak out against bad ideas. You can do something like this in an email, newsletter, or even presentation and see who is willing to say it's a bad idea. They're likely to give you some good ideas in the process.

Once you've identified your team, you will want them to map out what the customer experience is for your products and services. This is one area where it would help to have a Lean Startup or Lean Operations practitioner help you out by asking all the dumb questions that your team won't necessarily think are relevant.

After you have mapped out the customer experience as it is now (the current state), you will ask your team to develop a much better, idealistic future state

---

43. Note: Sometimes the person with the great idea has no idea how to manage the idea; they just like throwing them out there and seeing what happens. Make sure you have people in place who want to take the ideas and develop them. This is something I've learned by facilitating workshops, consulting, and coaching others who have a new idea every minute—they need guidance on how to help develop the idea into reality, otherwise the ideas are just a dime a dozen!

where everything up and down that value chain is better for your customers. This is where you, as the leader, are of the utmost importance—not because of what you will do, but rather because of what you won't do.

DON'T INTERFERE!

Your job is to, once again, empower these people to think as freely and creatively as they can. You want them to develop the most perfect model they can without limitations or restrictions. Most managers are very good at limiting scopes and saying what can't be done. Your job is to ensure they challenge what is being done to create what others would think is either impractical or impossible.

Once they've mapped this out (which should take weeks, not months or years), you will ask them to prepare a presentation for you and your executive team, along with a few customers if you're brave enough, to tell everyone what the customer experience should look like in your business.

Be brave! It's likely going to be a tough pill to swallow when they poke holes in all the ways you are currently losing customers or missing opportunities.

You will hopefully be impressed with the new and creative ways these people see you servicing your customers. You will likely also be confused because their vision for your business and yours may not jive. That's okay. It's still your business and your call, but you will now have input from some of your best people on how to start making that vision a reality.

Next, you need to validate some of their ideas. Again, your ZOG is to lead and empower a high-performing team, so they need to go out there and speak with customers to validate their hypotheses. (If this sounds familiar, it's because these same strategies work to build a new company altogether.)

If they start working with real customers to gather real feedback on their ideas, they will either find they're on the right track or that they've completely missed the mark. There will seldom be a time when they are 100 percent spot on, because they likely aren't aware of all the intricacies customers face when making decisions to work with you.

Again, that's okay. The intent here is to start mapping out a better way to provide products and services your customers want.

The last step is to test the ideas. I'd love to say this is easy, but it can be anything but. After they've validated, modified, or thrown out some ideas, the team will need to reconvene the executive team to propose a process improvement project.

My suggestion is to create a "skunkworks" type of setup rather than attempt to roll out a broad restructuring. Any type of change at this magnitude results in blowback and even outright sabotage if people don't know why they are doing it or don't believe it will work.

Instead, let your team assemble a few people to test their ideas in a small segment, separate from the rest of the business. Don't let the rest of the company know you're working on something new. Don't make big announcements to the press or your customers. Instead, just have periodic meetings set up with the team to check on the progress.

The assessment of whether or not the project is successful depends on two things, which can actually be measured by one thing: Money!

Your two criteria for success should be:

1. Customer satisfaction

2. Increased revenue

The one measurement of success is simply **Customer Lifetime Value**.[44] If your team creates new processes, products, or services that do not increase the

---

44. Explained in great depth in my training, which you can find at www.AngelNetwork.com/bonus

value of each customer to the organization by yielding more revenue and more profitability, then it likely isn't worth pursuing. If, however, you find

1. The customers' average purchase price has increased,

2. The number of repeat purchases has increased, AND

3. The number of customers profitably acquired increases

Then you can rest assured that customer satisfaction has increased. Instead of spending several months and several thousand (or million) dollars on net promoter scores or customer satisfaction polling consultants, you can simply look at how your customers are spending their money.

Customers vote with their wallets, and if they're voting more, more often, and you're getting more voters, then that's a clear win. Of course, getting quick feedback is vital to a continuous improvement process, so you will want some sort of feedback mechanism, as outlined in a previous chapter.

The rollout and implementation process outlined here is only possible when your employees are on board. This isn't a book on change management or organizational theory, so I will instead outline my philosophy on how to get the buy in from your employees so they will embrace this change.

Study after study has shown that when people feel valued in their role, they are more likely to stay in that role and put in the effort. When people stop feeling valued, they don't care about benefit packages, salaries, or the other items you might think they do. They don't care how big the carrot is that you dangle in front of them if reaching out to get it isn't in some way helping them feel better about doing so.

If you've hired good people over the years, those people want to feel valued. If you place an emphasis on providing superior customer service, then you need to empower your employees to provide that service. When you implement policies and procedures that make it impossible for them to service the customer, or you don't show your appreciation to your employees for providing great service, then you won't have a truly customer-centric operational model for long.

If you treat your employees right, then they will treat your customers right. That is all it really boils down to.

Do the Right Thing![45]

---

45. Yes, this needs a footnote. Many people struggle with what the "right" thing is to do in a given situation. Here are my ideas: 1) Don't cause harm; 2) Serve first, be served last; 3) Give everything, expect nothing; 4) Be honest and transparent; 5) Lift others up; and 6) Don't ignore people not doing the right thing because you are afraid—confront the situation head on.

Chapter Twenty-One
Putting It All Together

Getting your dolphins on board a submarine is quite a process, and vital to the overall success of any submarine. The process of becoming qualified in submarines, known among submariners as *earning your dolphins*, is a humbling and frustrating process for most.

It starts nearly the first day you walk onboard the boat. "Nub" and "Nonquals" or non-qualified sailors aboard a submarine are a form of subhuman species that exists only to clean and do all the crappy jobs that qualified submariners prefer not to do. Their lot in life is relegated to staying awake for an obscene number of hours and spending every spare minute they aren't cleaning with their nose in an operating manual learning everything they can about the submarine, its systems, and their role therein.

As I read the journal I kept during my first deployment years prior, all I could think about was how much I complained and lamented my own position on the boat. My frustrations as a junior unqualified sailor were those of cleaning the same valves, pipes, and bilges day after day without any end in sight. The dust bunnies continued to build, and I didn't understand the purpose in receiving 18-24 months of nuclear power training and education to become an overqualified janitor.

As I read the entries I made about the mundane existence I had back then, all I could think about was how narrow my field of vision was to the greater picture. I didn't understand at that time that there really was a process to the education I was receiving. The humbling humiliation I received when I didn't understand how the vertical launch system worked or what the process was to come to periscope depth further fueled my frustration at cleaning every nook and cranny on the boat.

Years later, as a division leader and watch supervisor, I could clearly see the reasoning behind every evolution we put our junior personnel through. The discipline of cleaning and maintaining well-polished equipment ensured the equipment would operate as needed in a time of emergency. Sticking my nose in manuals and countless volumes of engineering and nontechnical manuals helped me understand better where my role intersected with the remainder of the crew.

It wasn't until real situations came up (such as the potential sinking of our entire boat that I outlined in chapter sixteen) that all the training began to make sense. When a fire erupted in our dryer from someone not properly cleaning out the lint screen and keeping the coils free of combustible material, I fully adopted the Navy's preventive maintenance and qualification procedures wholeheartedly.

When you are on a submarine, the two things you fear most are a breach of the SUBSAFE[46] boundary that protects you from the ocean, and fire. When our dryer caught on fire, one of my friends almost immediately noticed the smoke coming out, and without hesitation radioed in the situation, grabbed an extinguisher, and promptly stopped the blaze. Within those few seconds, the entire boat had mobilized and prepared itself for what could have been a life-threatening situation. Smoke had already begun filling the forward compartment, and the distinct smell had wafted throughout the boat.

Procedures were implemented immediately and without question to bring the boat to periscope depth and begin ventilating the compartment and clearing the smoke. Our Emergency Air Breathing (EAB) masks were handed out from the sailors nearest the stowage compartments, and without a second thought, we donned our gear.

---

46. The SUBSAFE program is specific to submarines to a ensure lack of quality in workmanship or material doesn't result in a catastrophic failure that could sink the boat. Only two U.S. Navy nuclear submarines have sunk: the USS *Thresher* (SSN-593) and the USS *Scorpion* (SSN-589).

It was in those few moments that the benefit of all the training, cleaning, and humiliation finally set in. The humility is a byproduct of knowing you are not as smart as you thought you were—not the main intent of the qualification process. The reason sailors (or any military personnel, for that matter) are so passionate about making sure everyone understands their job and the job of the person next to them is because there is no room or time for error. There is nowhere to run. There is nothing to do but get the job done in the swiftest way possible.

That cannot be done without every hand on board knowing what must be done in any emergency. That is the point of qualifying aboard a submarine: to help sailors understand the important role they play not just in their own job, but as a member of the crew.

You are a band of brothers aboard a submarine, even if you don't necessarily like the guy in the rack next to you. When that man wears dolphins on his chest, you know that no matter how much you dislike him personally, you can count on him to do what needs to be done to save your ass and everyone else's if everything goes wrong, and he can count on you to do the same.

The sailor who failed to do his job and clean the lint trap that day or follow procedures when starting the dryer will never forget. I guarantee he has never made that mistake again and has even gone on to be one of the loudest voices echoing the call to get all junior personnel qualified and understanding the importance of following procedures. By forcing each person to earn their dolphins, the Navy fosters a culture of camaraderie and support, not one of malicious intent to humiliate junior personnel.

The point is, that unless you have everyone in your business understanding the importance of their role and how they personally are vital to the success and growth of your business, you will constantly risk losing everything. When your receptionist takes a blasé attitude toward answering the phones, greeting personnel at the front door, or assisting others within the office, it is simply a reflection on how well you have trained your staff to understand their importance.

Throughout this book, you've learned a little about how the engine room of a submarine works, as well as how military operations, leadership, and systems can impact the growth of a business. At the core of it all is the underlying assumption that you and everyone in your business is doing something that matters.

Time after time, studies have shown that people are not simply motivated by paychecks, but moreso for being recognized for the value they provide to their organization. When they feel they have value, they will work harder and do their job to the best of their abilities.

The challenge is that we don't have time to answer every challenge, problem, or question that arises from our staff 24/7. We can't possibly be involved in every situation that would require senior level support. Nor can we always predict what challenges will arise as we try to grow a business.

So how then can we grow a business if we can't possibly prepare for every situation? How can we help our staff answer questions that would further elevate the company's success?

The answer has been scattered throughout this book, directly and indirectly. If you chose to skim and just happened to find this chapter without having picked up all the points along the way, here it is:

A business designed for growth and success constantly implements systems, processes, and procedures to help its staff provide the best possible service to its customers AND relentlessly improves every aspect of these components and its people!

Most business owners, CEOs, entrepreneurs, and executives don't adopt a relentless pursuit of perfection in everything they do, and certainly don't hold their staff to that standard as well. As a result, they are far behind the curve when it comes to innovating and growing their business.

They realize far too late that customer loyalty has dipped or that their products and services are no longer satisfactory in the current marketplace. The purpose behind designing systems, processes, and procedures, AND WRITING THEM DOWN, is that you don't have the time or the ability to be involved in every aspect of the business. For that reason, you must adopt a mentality of continuous improvement in all areas.

However, you can't hope to improve on something that doesn't exist!

You must start with the foundation and put basic procedures in place for handling the most common situations.

- How should everyone answer the phone?[47]

- What are the sales processes that everyone should be aware of?

- How do you help a customer purchase from you? (Seems like a silly thing to ask, but try asking all of your staff how customers buy more and more often from your business—you might be surprised!)

- What is the procedure for answering customer complaints?

- How does management get informed when customers are asking for services you don't currently offer? (This is how you find new opportunities for your business, so you need it in place!)

- Is there a right and wrong way to send emails?

- How do you communicate with your customers about upcoming sales?

- How do you communicate with your staff about promotions before they occur?

---

47. Seriously. The scripts should be developed for every single situation. You should even have process flows mapped out for the responses you get from customers. Don't gloss over this. Failure to do this could be the difference between single digit growth (or worse, a decline) and doubling your business!

These are just some basic questions you should be asking and using to develop processes and procedures. Then you design systems around these best practices to ensure you get the results you want consistently at every level in the organization!

In the resources section, I list some of my favorite tools for implementing some of these processes and procedures, and in my training and consulting programs I provide clients with templates they can use to build their businesses faster.

If you're curious about how you can start implementing these same processes and procedures in your business, or need help customizing systems for your business, implementing processes or procedures, or coaching and training your teams, visit www.AngelNetwork.com to find out how we can help you.

Chapter Twenty-Two
Startup, Innovate, Operate

Building a business takes time. Building a great business takes discipline.

However, there is a procedure you can use to start, build, operate, innovate, and grow a business of any kind. Every business starts with an idea. From there, the leader inspires people to action, who in turn work on making the vision come to life.

As they do this, best practices are either developed or found, and systems are created to build on those best practices. This allows you to operate your business seamlessly, fulfilling the promises you made to the customer when they handed you their hard-earned money.

As you operate, you stagnate if you aren't focused on getting better, which is why you innovate. Constantly look at everything you are doing from the top to the bottom and find new ways to make your business better.

As you continue, your team gets excited about change or they leave. The ones who leave simply aren't prepared for the next phase of growth, which is okay. Instead, grow by bringing in better people who are better suited for the next phase of your business.

At every turn, ask this one question, and you will constantly be ahead of your competition:

> *"How Do We Do This Better Tomorrow Than We Did Yesterday?"*[48]

The more you ask this one question, the faster you will grow.

Starting a business isn't hard. In fact, starting is the easy part. Getting your first customer can be daunting, and your first $100,000 in revenue will be you hardest hundred grand. Most small businesses never scale beyond that level because they fail to proceduralized what works and instead spend every day reinventing the wheel.

You won't have to do that if you keep asking the question above and then putting best practices in place to innovate and accelerate the ways in which you provide value to your customers.

I've been lucky enough to start and work in several businesses that have gone from concept to over $500k, coached entrepreneurs who have created multi-million dollar businesses, and consulted and worked with many businesses that have single clients worth $50 Million or more per year, so I know what it takes to go through the various stages of a business. However, most founders stagnate in the startup phase which focuses on relentless innovation and customer acquisition without standardizing processes.

Big businesses stagnate when they rely only on their aging systems and processes and newcomers out-innovate them.

The companies that outshine their competition are those that maintain a certain culture of entrepreneurialism and continue to innovate on their ideas while instilling best practices and systems wherever possible to ensure maximum value is being provided to their customers.

---

48. Ask this question until the answers seem absurd. Once they seem absurd, you will have a much better idea of what the future might look like. Then you reverse-engineer that and you improve your processes to make them even better.

If you are doing this correctly, it means you will never run out of new ideas to test. This is the name of the game in business growth. You cannot grow if you keep doing things the same way you always have been.

The beauty of doing this is that you start creating new revenue streams that may even replace and eclips your original revenue source. But you must be sure that you have the right structure and systems in place before you begin to implement new services or deliver new products.

But what does that really mean? Let's discuss examples in the next chapter.

Chapter Twenty-Three
Optimize & Innovate

"For Christ's sake! Every damn time I turn on the fucking computer I about have an aneurism, epileptic seizure, and stroke at the same fucking time! Just the thought of looking at that stupid fucking program again makes me have a panic attack! And I used to smoke sitting on top of a fifty-gallon barrel of fuel oil!"

In many businesses, a tirade like this would result in an immediate pink slip or at least a trip to the principal's office (i.e. HR).

I just called it Monday.

Our company had invested several million dollars in a computer program aimed at increasing our operational efficiency and reducing our overall costs. The slogan "we optimize for the whole, not the individual" was regularly repeated among IT and management ranks alike.

On the deck plate level though, the sentiment was slightly more…agitated, to put it nicely.

"You know how we could get more efficient, Barnes? Get rid of the whole fucking thing, ask us to use the yellow pages, Thomas Guide, and a unicycle to get around!"

Honestly, I could hardly disagree. As a manager, leader, and coach for my employees, my first and only thought on my position was that I should do everything in my power to enable them to do everything in their power to service the customers.

Unfortunately, I spent nearly half of my time trying to "defend" a broken software system. And I couldn't even do that with a straight face.

The challenge was—and this is true of every large company I've worked with or for—that the managers making decisions from the control room hadn't been down to the deck plate in quite some time…if ever!

If you want to continue to scale a company that is already at the eight, nine, or even ten-figure mark, then you have no choice but to transform and do things in a whole new way. Building cars today the way Henry Ford did—not in concept, but the same way—would result in a bankrupt company before the first sale.

Managers making decisions from the control room hadn't been down to the deck plate in quite some time…if ever!

This makes sense, right? You can't embark on a journey of transformation without adopting new systems, tools, or technology, and that is true now more than ever.

However, there is a very important formula that I have developed and found to be incredibly true in every transformation project, and its simplicity can't be overstated or ignored.[49]

OPTIMIZATION

Once you implement the ideas listed earlier in this book, you will begin to have systems, processes, and procedures that you can rely on to get your customers taken care consistently and with dependability.

---

49. I've covered this in several areas in this book with different words to describe the same goal. If you need help implementing this in your business, head over to www.AngelNetwork.com/bonus to learn more.

However, as tools and technology evolve, or as customers begin to demand new services or products, minor adjustments must be made to ensure their continued satisfaction and patronage.

It also means that you must be continuously looking at all these processes from the ground up and ensuring they are improved upon. The *Kaizen* principles apply here more than anywhere else in your business.

Failure to optimize your processes results in failing to keep pace with change, and thus risking the loss of good paying customers. One such example would be Amazon's same-day delivery of everything from an LED Toilet Night Light (yes, that's a real thing) to the ginger for your juicer in the morning. In our on-demand society, people have stopped planning weeks in advance for, well, anything, and thus we need everything today; Amazon along with several other companies is answering that call.

Here's one important caveat to keep in mind at all times:

Optimization must always be a ground-up approach that focuses first on the customer's needs, not the company's!

If you decide that you just want to improve, say, the office layout for your IT floor, it had better be because you want your teams to work better together and have more room for collaboration—otherwise, what are you doing? Creating a "properly branded" floor layout "commensurate with company standards, policy go suck an egg…" is absurd, yet it is what people spend time and money discussing.

How does the customer benefit?

INNOVATION

Ah yes, the buzzword of the decade…Innovation.

Everyone wants to be innovative.

"Our brand new state-of-the-art microwave with Bluetooth capability to let you know when your popcorn is actually done will save you the frustration and agony of knowing when three minutes is actually up, if you happen to walk more than ten feet away from your microwave!"

Fucking stupid!

Yet that's the way so many people look at innovation. The next shiny object or catchy doodad that can be attached to an already extraneous piece of crap.

Do I sound cynical? If so, it's because I am.

My job for the past several years has been to politely tell people their ideas aren't worth a hill of beans.

My role as an innovation coach, consultant, speaker, and facilitator more often than not boils down to bringing people back to reality. They haven't even considered who has the problem they're trying to solve or why it should be solved before they begin.

"We'll monetize the data." Fluff for "We have no fucking clue how we'll make money with this idea, but I'm sure someone will buy it!"

"Our goal is to acquire one million users prior to developing a revenue model so that we don't disrupt the user's experience." In other words, "We love our idea so much that we're willing to risk and lose all of our investors' money to prove that one million other idiots will like our idea too!"

Here's the thing—innovation for innovation's sake is a stupid game. It's the new-age version of trying to fit the square peg in the round hole.

Just trying to "one-up" your competition is absurd. Innovation, when done correctly, does one thing and one thing only…

It improves someone's life in a *meaningful* way.

Back up cameras—genius! No more running over the bike the kid left out...or worse, the bike with the kid on it!

The ability to break down a synthetic material that is lighter and stronger than carbon steel, that was previously not recyclable, and which costs 50 percent less to produce without harming the environment? Great!

The ability to help vehicles communicate with each other faster than humans can respond to avoid fatal or costly motor vehicle accidents? Perfect!

Creating a motor to go in a skateboard because using your foot is too "old school"? Seriously?

Unless, of course, you are just proving that a motor the size of your hand is capable of record-setting speeds and could be the next generation of public transportation...then it might be worth testing.

In case you're wondering, these are all ideas that entrepreneurs have actually come up with and, yes, I have worked on with them.

I could write an entire book on innovation, and maybe I will someday, but for now suffice it to say that innovation should simply solve an existing problem that more than one person has, and it should be a meaningful problem. If you're a business owner or executive and you want to change the world, don't focus your time and energy on useless innovation.

Focus instead on solving a significant problem that people need help with.

TRANSFORMATION

Your business five years from now should not look remotely the same as it does today. Perhaps the core vision or even deliverable is unaltered, but the tools and technology you use to provide those services need to change and adapt.

However, if you simply go down the path of transforming your business because your CEO, CIO, or CFO thinks it's a good idea after they read some book or blog, then you might be going down the rabbit hole as our company did with the software snafu that opened this chapter.

A company should only transform because it believes it is in the customers' best interest. Not the C-suite, not the shareholders, not even the employees...

THE CUSTOMERS!

If what you are doing is not going to have a meaningful, lasting, positive impact on your customers, then just stop.

It doesn't make sense to focus on minor or short-lived innovations or transformation. Of course, you won't always know if it will be a spark that fades before it catches anything on fire, or a wildfire ready to blaze until you put it into action, but you can attempt to answer most of those questions before you get started.

That's the topic of another book, and we'll just leave it there for now. Perhaps I'll include some ideas on innovation and transformation in my bonuses at www.AngelNetwork.com/bonus. Just not sure right now...

THE PERPETUAL CYCLE

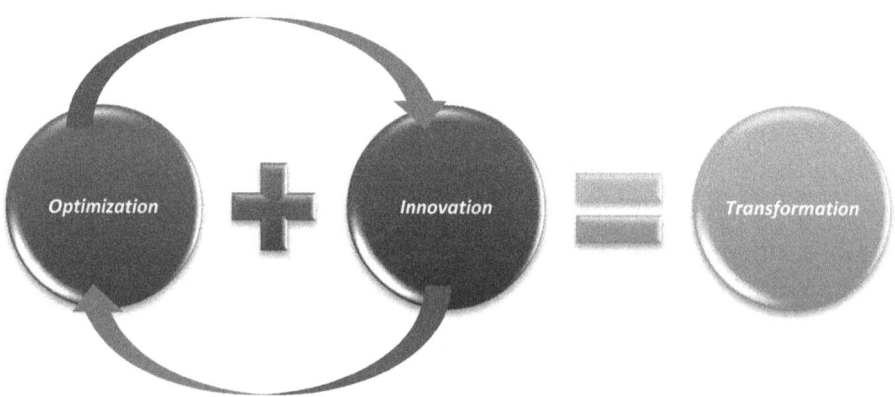

Why the arrows in the equation?

Optimization and innovation are two parts of the same process. You literally cannot have one without the other. You cannot attempt to innovate on a new product or service without in some way affecting the operations, sales, finance, or customer service aspect of the existing company.

Therefore, the company must remain agile and able to respond to these changes regularly. In some cases, companies go through several iterations of optimization every year due to new ideas that breed even more new ideas.

In James Altucher's book *Choose Yourself*, he goes into great detail about coming up with new ideas and how these new ideas breed even more ideas. His phrasing is pretty fun, so I'll repeat it here.

Altucher states that your ideas begin to have sex and produce offspring that will continue to add value to your own career, business, and the world.

There is a tremendous power in implementing many of the strategies and tactics I've outlined in this book, but the most powerful of all is having an open line of communication to your team and company so you can generate and implement new ideas!

I can't stress this enough – businesses stagnate and fall behind when they fail to implement new ideas on a consistent basis. If you want to succeed and scale, you must be trying new ideas all the time.

This is of course impossible if your structure, your foundation, your core principles and values, and of course your systems aren't already well-tuned.

In short, if you aren't already operating your core business like a well-oiled machine, innovation and transformation will be unlikely at best.

Chapter Twenty-Four
Conclusion

This book took me a little longer to write than I'd hoped, but such is life with two businesses, two kids, and a ton of ideas. I'm publishing an imperfect manuscript knowing that as soon as I do there will be more I want to change or add, but better to publish and move on than to get stuck in the never-ending cycle of change for change's sake.

So instead of pondering what else I need to add or waiting for another great idea to come knocking, I'm going to conclude now by saying thank you.

Thank you, sincerely, for reading this, my extended soapbox speech on how to transform your business and in doing so change the world.

I want to let you know that I continue to write about, speak about, and work with companies on all the ideas contained in this book, among many others. In fact, I've created a couple short pages in the Appendices to explain how I might continue to be of service to you after you put down this book.

So, again, thank you and I hope to hear from you someday about how this book impacted you or your business! Until then, Jeff Barnes, signing off!

Jeff Barnes, Former MM1 (SS/DV)[50]
The Submariner Business Consultant

---

50. MM1: Machinist's Mate, First Class, my rate. SS: Qualified in Submarines. DV: Qualified Scuba Diver.

Appendix One
Nine Nuclear Navy Principles

As my career has progressed, I have found it important to adopt principles that would help me filter out bad ideas and processes to reach my goals faster. I named these the Nine Nuclear Navy Principles because they all are somehow rooted in my experiences in the Navy. Please note that these are not the Navy's principles, but rather mine based on what I learned while serving aboard the USS *Jefferson City*.

These principles have helped me in every area, not the least of which is attracting like-minded people to me and repelling those who would not be a good fit as a customer, employee, peer, or friend. I believe this is important in helping define who we are and what we stand for, and so these principles remain core to my beliefs in how I live my life and manage my businesses.

Feel free to adopt, modify, use, or throw out any or all of them as these are mine, and yours are likely to be different.

1. THERE IS ONLY ONE DECISION-MAKER

> *"The worst of all human ailments is indecision!"*
>
> *~Napoleon Hill, 1883-1970*

In almost every situation I can recall where poor or no decisions were made to make meaningful change, I can cite one common theme: too many decision-makers and no one having the final say.

In one such instance, a CEO I know failed to enforce a global mandate for adopting one software program because the executives of his business units bickered and dragged on about how that one software wasn't "perfect" for their situation. So, after thousands of man-hours wasted, no decision was made; three years later, the business hadn't made any significant change and was back to the drawing board.

If you are in charge, then it is up to you to decide. People will criticize you no matter what decision you make, so just make one. You will never please everyone, so use your experience and intuition and decide. While it is important to heed the advice of experts and get opinions from those closest to the matter, it is imperative that you do not allow a committee to make the final determination. Let them present ideas, and then you must act.

If you are not the decision-maker, then you must force the hand of the person from whom you need support. Do not allow them to waffle back and forth. Countless hours and resources are wasted by indecision.

Decide and move on. There are very few decisions that cannot be changed or corrected in the future. Even when dealing with a nuclear power plant, we had one person who could trump everyone else and didn't need to convene a committee.

2. There Will Be Accountability

Too often, people can coast by without being held accountable. One of the biggest fears people have is being wrong, so they choose not to act. Since no action is taken, no progress is made. If no progress is made, what's the point?

Conversely, if you insist on progress, you must hold people accountable. If you are going to hold people accountable, they must have the ability to decide (see #1). If you find that people are not taking action regularly and believe they aren't being properly held accountable, then you need to learn how to empower them to act and decide without getting your blessing.

Give people a target at which to aim and a gun with bullets, and they can generally figure out the rest. Tell somebody to just shoot something without any direction, and you're likely to get a messy result. This is how most people manage and lead, and they wonder why nothing happens. Most will not want to be held accountable without knowing what the expectations are.

Set the expectations, create goals, and then hold people to them. Then you will see progress.

3. There Will Be Deadlines

If you want action, and progress, you must make decisions and hold people accountable. The best way to ensure things get done is to set deadlines. Almost every so-called expert on the process of setting and achieving goals tells you that having a deadline is critically important.

Assigning responsibilities is no different. Each task is considered a goal, and each one must have a clear deadline.

If a general told his colonels to set up camp and get ready to engage the enemy "sometime soon," how likely is it they would be ready and able to combat the enemy? Highly unlikely, right?

The same goes with company mandates. If you want to achieve a goal, you need a deadline. If you are the leader, your goals are bigger and result in many other people focusing on smaller items. Your big goal needs a deadline so everyone below you can work backwards from that date and create timelines, strategies, and tactics to achieve their goals in time to help you reach yours.

4. There Will Be Written Down, Clearly Defined Standard Operating Procedures

No surprise here, I should think. But here's why I focus on SOPs so much: you can't always find the perfect player for each position.

Not only that, but people have off days. You and I both have bad days where our brains are in a fog or something else is on our minds.

If you have critical tasks that must be achieved on a frequent basis, then the only guarantee you have of achieving those tasks and goals is having standard operating procedures in place.

The greatest benefit of having SOPs in place is that it allows you to assess the skills and abilities that the person performing those SOPs must possess to be effective in that role. If you are simply guessing at what the role requires, then you are placing bets on hope and luck that the person you hire will be able to fulfill that role the way you want.

Once an SOP is developed, it needs to be fluid to allow changes if there is a better way to achieve the result. However, it cannot be "tribal knowledge"—that information that is simply stored in the heads of your longtime employees and not written down anywhere.

To learn more on how to develop SOPs, go back and reread chapters 12-16, or visit www.AngelNetwork.com to watch a free training on how to develop your own.

5. THERE WILL BE MANDATORY AND ONGOING TRAINING & QUALIFICATIONS

The training process to become a "nuc" in the Navy takes anywhere from sixteen to twenty-four months of pure classroom and hands-on training in a safe environment. Afterwards, when a sailor heads to sea for the first time, they must then train and qualify even further for their specific role.

All told, it can take upwards of two and a half years for some individuals to finally start doing the work they were originally hired to do. That is, of course, an extreme case, yet the same should be true for anyone in a highly skilled position.

Unfortunately, many businesses and managers rely on "on the job" training as a benchmark for doing one's job, and they don't properly track and manage this process. If your newest employee simply gets some on the job training

(OJT) from the jerk-off who bad-mouths the boss and "corporate" all day long, how likely is it that your newest employee will a) like his new job, and b) be any good at it?

If you want to position your company for growth and success, you must train people properly and then test their level of knowledge and skills to ensure they properly acquired the skillset you need in that role. This is true whether you're hiring your receptionist or a highly compensated computer software developer.

Train people, qualify them, set expectations and deadlines, implement procedures, and then empower employees to make decisions that will benefit the company, and I promise you'll start seeing results.

6. NO EXCUSES!

If you have children, then you are probably already on board with this one. If you're a CEO, entrepreneur, or business owner, then you're probably good with this one too.

But how likely is it that your employees, coworkers, vendors, contractors, or even children live by this mantra?

Doubtful, right?

But what if that was a rule in your business? What if you could have a conversation with someone who didn't complete the task assigned to them, and the response you got was "I'm sorry. I have no excuse"?

You might be a little ticked off, but more than likely the next words out of that person's mouth will be "It won't happen again."

If you employ a no excuses policy, it doesn't mean that everything must be done correctly 100 percent of the time. Instead, what you are broadcasting to the company is that you are okay if things go wrong from time to time, but that you won't let people simply point the finger or place blame elsewhere. Refer to principle #2: There Will Be Accountability!

7. Everyone Must Give a Damn!

This might very well be the hardest principle to live by and implement, but is the one that, if adopted, will make all the other principles much easier to live by.

Complacency is the killer of progress. People get complacent because they either think they know it all too well and don't need to pay as much attention or they just don't give a shit anymore.

When you have a company or a military unit filled with people who just don't care about the mission, vision, or achieving any goals, it is all but impossible to have a successful outcome.

Conversely, even if you have the worst processes, no accountability, and very little structure in place, if you have a team of highly motivated and enthusiastic people working together because they care about the cause or vision, then you are much more likely to succeed.

It's hard to hire this trait, but I suggest you start with figuring out what you want your culture to be, what your vision is, and what your purpose for building your company is before you just ask people if they would care to work for you.

8. There Will Be Teams!

There's no such thing as a self-made man or woman. Never has been, never will be.

Similarly, there's no company that has ever existed that achieved any sort of success that was built 100 percent by one person. Teams help us achieve goals faster and easier and provide a better perspective than one person can alone.

However, there must be rules in place for teams. For one, there must be one person who is empowered to be the team's final decision-maker or swing vote. Refer to #1.

Second, the team should be as small as possible while still incorporating the right stakeholder segments. I'd suggest no more than six people in most cases, but this isn't an absolute.

9. Work Hard, Play Hard!

So many people say this, but they don't live it. It isn't the words that matter, it's the execution.

To build a great business, you need to rely on people to perform more tasks than can be accomplished by one person. To rely on people, you need to build a certain amount of trust in those people. You must be confident in their abilities, and they must be confident in yours.

Trust and rapport are not built by hanging out in a cubicle next to someone for months on end and having water-cooler chats. They also aren't built at weekend retreats once a year to learn how to work as a team.

In a submarine, you are forced to live with your coworkers for months on end. You learn more about them than you ever wanted to in some cases, but it helps you develop a bond.

Then, when you are in port, everyone heads out to the bars and clubs together to blow off steam. I have been in situations where I've been sharing a beer and a story with guys who are the biggest assholes to work with, but we left work on the sub. We also knew that, because we had similar ideals and principles like those laid out here, we could inherently trust each other and have each other's backs, even if we weren't best friends.

This camaraderie and trust is what helps companies grow to be great at what they do. It helps people love the work they do, not necessarily because it is a great job or even the most exciting industry, but because they love working side-by-side with the people next to them.

Remember, work isn't the goal. Being fulfilled and helping others is, and our businesses and jobs help us achieve that goal.

But why not enjoy the people you work with while you're at it?

Appendix Two
Resources

SYSTEMS TO GROW YOUR BUSINESS
SALES & MARKETING

ClickFunnels: Build your websites using this CRM software to automate the process flow of customers looking for you all the way through purchase, upsell, and relationship building. Also has an email marketing component called Actionetics to help you automate the entire marketing process.

Infusionsoft: Designed specifically to send out sequenced email or offline marketing messages and segment customer lists.

Social Media Marketing: Facebook for Business, LinkedIn, Twitter, YouTube, etc.

Online Marketing: Google AdWords, AdSense, various display advertising networks.

Mailing Lists: Standard Rates and Data Service (SRDS).

PAYROLL

ADP: Can set up small business accounts for your business, employees can log time via an app, and you can approve payroll instantly from your phone. Plus it handles most of the tax filings.

Wave: Online bookkeeping and accounting software that can create and send invoices, monitor bank accounts and credit card transactions, and make categorizing finances easy.

QuickBooks: But if you are big enough for QuickBooks or something similar, outsource or hire a CPA to manage it for you.

Project Management

Trello: Free online visual project management tool to help you determine next steps and create assignments.

Slack: Online group collaboration and communication tool that can help you keep tabs on where projects are and provide an easy place to house communications.

MS Visio: More robust and advanced project management tool geared toward project management pros.

Smart Draw: This tool allows you to develop flow charts, floor plans, layouts, swim lanes, GANTT charts, and so many other simple designs that will help you better communicate your ideas to your team.

Process & Procedure Development

The best tool I have found for this so far is Microsoft's OneNote. This tool allows you to constantly update and share all processes and procedures and helps you gather best practices from your staff. It can also be used as an onboarding tool if you have fully documented your various procedures. Think of it like an online Employee Handbook that can be easily updated.

File Sharing and Collaboration

Any of these resources can be helpful, but they all require you to spend some time setting up and creating useful file structures:[51]

---

51. Please note that these services were all fully functioning and operational at the time of this writing, but anything can change at any time in this world, so don't curse my name if they aren't around when you read this book!

- MS SharePoint

- Dropbox

- MS OneDrive

- iCloud

- Hightail (this one is great for sharing very large files)

- Google Drive and Google Docs

MANAGEMENT TOOLS

If you need help becoming better at managing people, of course it helps to know how you interact with people and how your staff interacts with you. Remember, we manage systems and lead people, and the best leaders are the ones who are greatest at finding and keeping the best talent.

- Sally Hogshead's *How the World Sees You* is a great book you might want to pick up. Take her Fascination Test at www.HowToFascinate.com.

- Peter Drucker is considered by many to be the top management guru around. If you've never managed people before, or just want to get better, then pick up his books or courses.

- DISC Personality Profiling is useful in understanding how you make decisions and how your staff might do things differently. There are hundreds of DISC Profile Assessment companies, but Tony Robbins's is one I would recommend.

- Myers-Briggs personality assessments are like the DISC assessment but dive deeper into other areas that help explain your decision-making process. You should also invest in a Kolbe Assessment.

- Dashboards! No manager should ever wonder what is happening in their business, and the only way to manage what is happening is to have a simple 360-degree view of your business numbers and statistics. Since there are so many depending on your type of business, it is hard to recommend just one; however, ClickFunnels and Infusionsoft (mentioned earlier) are great ways to manage the sales and marketing aspects of your business. Find others that are industry-specific for you to manage the operations.

Appendix Three
Coaching

For the past several years, I've coached dozens of entrepreneurs, business owners, and executives in the areas of

- Entrepreneurial principles
- Marketing & marketing strategies, specifically direct response
- Digital and online marketing
- Digital and mobile transformation
- Technology, systems, and tools
- Personal development and management
- Business development strategies

One of the greatest things about getting a coach is that we can see the limitations or obstacles much clearer and they will show you a path around them. The reason is that often we are too close to our own problems to see the solution right in front of our noses.

I especially like working with people who are in the same shoes I've been in—those entrepreneurial dreamers who still have a J-O-B. Nothing turns me off faster than some twenty-something kid who's never had a family, mortgage, or career trying to give advice on "how to achieve all of your dreams" if you just didn't have any of those obligations.

Let's be real—we can't all start the company of our dreams in our twenties, so instead we need actual strategies on how to move forward anyway, no matter our age.

If that sounds like something you'd be interested in, please head over to

www.AngelNetwork.com/bonus

to learn how you can start putting these ideas to work for yourself and even work with my team and me to help you get where you want to go sooner.

Appendix Four
Speaking

If you are looking for someone to speak at a conference, seminar, or to your group or company on the topics listed below, please head over to our site and let us know. The topics I prefer to speak the most about include

- Creating and scaling businesses, including business development

- Innovation and implementation

- Leadership

- Personal development

- Getting shit done! (Systems, processes, and procedures)

I'm available on a very limited basis for speaking on these topics and will be happy to discuss opportunities with you.

To fill out a form and request a call back for a speaking opportunity, please head over to www.JeffBarnes.CEO to learn more.

Appendix Five
Consulting

If your business is struggling with growth in this crowded and noisy market, then sometimes reading a book isn't good enough. Sometimes you need someone to come in and show you and your team what to do and give you the tools to help make it happen.

If that is something you are interested in, then please feel free to contact our company to set up a time to talk. Here are topics we can assist with either virtually or by on-site visits:

- Entrepreneurial and lean startup principles and workshops

- Design thinking projects

- Innovation processes and systems

- Innovation portfolio management

- Operational efficiency and optimization

- Customer service and service delivery

- Business development

- Business process improvement

- Marketing strategies and design

- Digital transformation and implementation

- Management systems

To set up a time to discuss a consulting engagement, please head over to www.JeffBarnes.ceo to learn more.

Glossary & Terms

In this section I will help you understand how sailors communicate and see the world. Please note that nothing in here is politically correct, and that is a true sign of a sailor—irreverent and full of piss and vinegar. At sea, your job isn't to make people happy or play nice. Your job is to get shit done and complete the mission. That doesn't mean they don't know how to tone it down around "civilians," but if you encounter a sailor, or more specifically a submariner, in his natural state, then you'll likely be offended and disgusted.

Take no offense—it's just how we deal with our world inside a 300-foot black tube hundreds of feet underwater in the middle of nowhere.

CAUTION: YOU WILL LIKELY BE OFFENDED, DISGUSTED, AND THINK VERY LITTLE OF ME IF YOU READ THIS SECTION...IF YOU'RE A CIVILIAN, THAT IS![52]

To my fellow submariners—forgive me for peeling back the curtain here, but you'll notice that I left out some terms that are reserved for the subs alone.

12-mile limit: Referring to the international twelve-mile boundary, but sailors use it to mark the time when "anything goes" while outside the twelve-mile limit.

"120 sailors go down, 60 couples come back": Derogatory phrase used by jealous surface sailors who think they are being funny. Ha fucking ha.

---

[52]. And I won't lose any sleep over it. If you don't like me, that's fine. Feel free to leave a negative review on Amazon if you wish. If you aren't offended yet, though, then this will only amuse you to no end! If you laugh here or anywhere else in this book, please leave a positive comment on Amazon to balance out the curmudgeons!

20 knots: The maximum speed of a submarine that is allowed to be told to someone outside the submarine community.

400 feet: The maximum depth of a submarine that is allowed to be told to someone outside the submarine community.

42 and a wake-up: Actually, any number and a wake-up. Counting down the days to going home, retirement, or any other significant event.

50-50-90: Term regularly used in the Nuclear Navy to explain that even when you have a 50-50 chance of answering a question correctly, you'll be wrong 90 percent of the time.

7 Ps: "Proper Prior Planning Prevents Piss-Poor Performance." Phrase usually found around any training facility. Also known as "Piss-Poor Planning Produces Piss-Poor Performance."

ADCAP: ADvanced CAPability. Latest version of the Mark 48 torpedo (as of this writing).[53]

"A failure to plan on your part does not constitute an emergency on mine!": Used when someone tries to assert their will over others because they didn't properly plan or sequence out their work. No special privileges, even for rank on submarines.

"Air in the banks, shit in the tanks, ready to submerge below...sound the diving alarm!": An abbreviated, unauthorized, yet humorous way to report the submarine is ready to dive.

---

53. Sometimes the Army, Marine Corps, and even Air Force like to play a little game and make fun of us sailors for never carrying weapons, and in some cases, never firing one. I earned my expert pistol and rifle marksmanship marks in the Navy, but the biggest weapon I ever got to fire was a 21-inch diameter, 19-foot long, 3,400+ pound torpedo for testing. Hooyah!

Ahead flank, cavitate!: To go fast without regard to how much noise you make. Usually done when being attacked by a torpedo, or more likely for testing or drills.

"All I need is a family-gram and a Diet Coke and I am happy to be underway": Usually said by a salty old submariner to a non-qual to indicate how dedicated they are.

Angles and dangles: The time when the submarine is making radical depth changes, pitches, and rolls. Usually done during sea trials and the pre-deployment underway period to ensure everything is stowed for sea properly.

Assholes and elbows: The only things that should be seen by a boatswain's mate when deck hands are on their hands and knees holystoning a wooden deck. Still used to indicate that during field day everyone should be cleaning and not goofing off.

A.T.F.Q.: Answer the fucking question.

A.T.Q.A.: Answer the question asked! In other words, stop rambling on trying to sound smart and just answer me!

Bagged: As in "I got bagged" by the off-going watch. Meaning you got left with something that someone else was supposed to do.

Baffles: The area immediately behind the submarine.

Balls to the wall: Flank speed.

Banging air: Running the high-pressure air compressor to charge the air banks.

Bent shitcan: Someone below Naval standards. "He's as fucked up as a bent shitcan."

Bilge: The bottom of the boat where all the grease, dust, grime, dirt, and other nasty fluids collect. Also, where the Gremlins live.

Bilge mole: The sailor designated to climb into the bilge whenever something needs to be retrieved because they can somehow contort their body into unusual shapes to get around and under pipes and equipment.

Bilge pickers: A long thin tool used to pick items out of out-of-reach areas. Also used by short people to get things out of high cupboards.

Blow and go: To emergency blow the main ballast tanks.

Blowing a shitter: Inadvertently "flushing" a toilet while sanitary tanks are being blown overboard. This causes excrement and toilet paper to be blown all over the head, to the delight of the rest of the crew.

Blow job: Emergency blow or emergency ventilate.

Blue nose: A person who has crossed the Arctic Circle and been initiated.

B.O.H.I.C.A.: Bend Over, Here It Comes Again. Referring to something bad about to happen again or as usual.

Boon dockers: The standard workday steel-toed boots.

Boondoggle: Any unorganized, inefficient evolution or a trip taken on government time and money.

Boy butter: Slang term for silicone grease.

Box of rocks: Derogatory term for a sailor who has performed their work in an unsatisfactory manner.

Brain fart: A condition when, under stress, one cannot recall or perform something that would normally be easy or second nature.

Bravo Zulu: Originally "BZ" was a signal meaning "Well Done." It is usually used by seniors to praise subordinates in one form or another.

Broach or **broaching the boat**: Sticking the sail of the submarine out of the water…a cardinal sin for a diving officer while underway. This is typically only intentionally done when preparing to surface; any other infraction (broach) while submerged could result in the submarine being detected.

Broke-dick: Technical term describing malfunctioning or inoperable equipment. Example: "The fuckin' aux drain pump is fuckin' broke-dick."

B.U.B.: Barely Useful Body.

Bubblehead: Internationally recognized term of endearment for a submarine sailor.

Buddy fucker: As implied, someone who fucks over their shipmates. Not to be trusted with any information of importance.

Bug juice: Kool-Aid-like beverage in dispensers on the mess decks. Before the turn of the century, bug juice was also used as a replacement for cleaning agents to clean decks with. Still used for removing corrosion from brass fittings.

B.U.F.F.: Big Ugly Fat Fucker.

Bullshit flag: An imaginary flag that someone "raises" when they believe that what someone is telling them is pure and utter bullshit. They will call out "I am raising the bullshit flag on that one," and in some cases sailors carry around a rag that they will throw on the ground as their bullshit flag.

Bumfuck, Egypt: BFE. A bad duty station or bad place in general. (Also funny—Bumfuck is somehow an allowed word per MS Word's dictionary!)

Bunk bag: They were originally elongated bags, designed for horizontal passageway storage and hung from the tubular bunk frames on diesel boats. In later years, they were hung inside racks and usually used for dirty clothes or to hide porn and patrol socks.

Bunkie: A term of endearment for your bed, bunk, or rack.

Burn a flick: Indicates to start the movie.

Burn run: An organized evolution to dispose of the classified material stored in burn bags.

Cadillac: A mop bucket, usually with wheels and a wringer.

Casino night: A night designated to play casino games such as poker, blackjack, etc. to raise money for the recreation committee.

Channel fever: Said if a sailor is anxious when approaching port to get leave.

Check valve: Also known as a "one-way check valve." A submariner who does things for himself but not for others.

Chasing the bubble: A term when the diving officer can't seem to trim off the boat right and the "bubble" (much like the bubble in a leveling tool) is riding up and down wildly, thus the boat is seesawing through the water.

Chicken switches: Emergency blow actuation valves. These are thrown to get the submarine to the surface to prevent sinking. Likely origination is from an old crusty sailor who thought it was a "chicken shit move" to blow to the surface rather than go down with the ship.

Chop: The supply officer. Taken from the Supply Corps' pork-chop-shaped insignia.

Clean sweep: Refers to having "swept the enemy from the seas," a completely successful mission. It is traditionally indicated by lashing a broom to the periscope of a submarine.

Clear your baffles: Look behind you…also known as "sweep the baffles."

"Close enough for horseshoes, hand grenades, or Polaris Missiles": A highly technical slang term used when a job is good enough to call complete. Also known as "Close enough for government work."

Cluster fuck: Refers to when a group performs some task in a severely disorganized manner, usually with poor results. May also be used to describe any person or thing that is in a state of general disarray. "That kid is a walking cluster fuck." Can be indicated using the NATO phonetic Charlie Foxtrot for CF.

C.O.B.: Chief of the Boat, or more affectionately, "Crabby Old Bastard." The senior enlisted person on board a submarine.

Coner: (CONE-err) A submarine crewman who is not part of the engineering department. Especially torpedo men, because they are stationed in the forward cone of the sub.

Cow: A refrigerated fixture in the galley that dispenses something like milk.

C.O.W.: Chief of the Watch. In charge of the ballast, air, and water systems while underway.

Countdown calendar: Used to count down the days until returning to port. Can be an actual calendar, chain made of paperclips, etc.

Crank: Mess deck worker, typically a new transfer to a submarine assigned to mess deck duties while qualifying for a regular watch. Also see NUB.

Cranial-rectal insertion: Having one's head up one's own ass.

Crazy Ivan: Demonstrated in the movie *The Hunt for Red October*. Russian submarines would quickly turn 180 degrees while underway to see whether any American submarines were following.

"**Damn, man, your voice has changed but your breath still smells the same**": Someone farted. Also heard as "Keep talking, Lieutenant, we'll find you."

Dick skinners: Your hands, e.g., "get your dick skinners off my white hat." Also known as Peter clamps, meat hooks, and dick beaters.

Dicking the dog: Putting a "half-assed" effort into a task. Refers to improperly securing the "dogs" on a watertight hatch when passing through. Such a lax procedure could spell doom for a sinking ship if hatches were not absolutely watertight. Also said as "poking the poodle." Not to be confused with "screwing the pooch," which refers to royally messing up a task.

D.I.L.L.I.G.A.F.: Does It Look Like I Give A Fuck? Universal acronym, but widely used in the Navy.

Dink or **Dinq**: Short for delinquent. See Dink List.

Dink check: Usually done just prior to movies and in areas where crewmembers might be relaxing. This was done to check that the area was clear of nonqualified crewmembers who were on the dink list (see below).

Dink list: Delinquent list. A list of nonqualified individuals who are not up to date on their qualification's status. In the older days of submarining, this was checked often, and a loss of privileges was afforded to anyone on the dink list.

Diver's 1MC announcement: "There are divers over the side, do not rotate screws, cycle rudders, take suction from or discharge to the sea, blow flood or vent any tanks, or operate any underwater equipment or activate sonar. There are divers over the side."

Dog and pony show: A special show put on for inspecting senior officers. Normally sailors are instructed not to ask questions of the senior officers, even if requested by the inspecting officer. Generally includes hours of uniform cleaning, tidying, ironing, and shoe polishing for a three-minute inspection of the crew.

Dolphins: Slang term for submarine warfare insignia worn only by those who have "qualified" in submarines…or those cute little swimmers that follow the submarine to sea.

Douche kit: Container (usually zipper-closed) for toilet articles such as shaving cream, deodorant, aftershave lotion, etc.

Double digit midget: A short timer. Someone who is less than 100 days from retirement, EAOS, being discharged to civilian life, or returning to port.

Drinking your dolphins: Extinct tradition. In the old submarine force, a time-honored tradition was to drink your dolphins if you were newly qualified. This consisted of your shipmates buying a shot of everything behind the bar and putting it all in a pitcher, dropping the dolphins into the pitcher, and the newly qualified submariner drinking until he caught his dolphins in his teeth. Unfortunately, incidents occurred from alcohol poisoning and injury from getting dolphins stuck in the throat, so the practice was officially banned.

EAB: Emergency Air Breathing. Akin to the fires of Hell, wearing this mask and going around plugging it in was/is a submariner's worst nightmare. Known as "sucking rubber," this mask could give you a headache and attitude adjustment in the worst way in just inside of thirty seconds. Making matters worse would be looking around at all the drill monitors not wearing theirs.

"Eat shit and bark at the moon": A phrase commonly used when someone doesn't like what someone else told them to do. As known as "fuck off and die" (F.O.A.D.).

E.S.A.D.: Eat Shit and Die.

E.W.A.G.: Engineered Wild Ass Guess or Educated Wild Ass Guess. Also see S.W.A.G.

Failed open: Used to describe when a person can't sleep and their eyes won't shut.

Family-grams: The one-way communication given to family before a submariner left on deployment. Family-grams changed over the years, but were usually limited to 20-50 words depending on operational priorities. Family-grams were sent from the loved one and were screened for anything that might upset the receiving submariner. They were usually read over and over and sometimes misinterpreted, causing much stress with the sailor.

F.A.T.A.S.S.: Fast Attack Tough and Super Salty.

Fat pill: A bread roll or cinnamon roll.

Fightin' gear: Eating utensils.

F.I.I.G.M.O.: Fuck It, I Got My Orders.

F.I.I.S.: Fuck It, I'm Short. Said by a sailor who's about to get out of the Navy and doesn't care anymore.

Finger wave: Prostate exam.

Firing point procedures: The announced point at which target motion analysis has been completed on a target and a solution has been generated to the point of preparing to shoot a torpedo. In reality, it is the time at which new weapons officers often reevaluate, overthink the solution, and make adjustments that will ultimately result in missing the target.

Fish: Torpedoes or submarine warfare qualification insignia.

Float test: To toss overboard.

F.L.O.B.: Freeloading Oxygen Breather. Someone who is not holding their own or carrying their share of the load. Usually a non-qual dink puke.

F.O.A.D.: Fuck Off and Die. Self-explanatory.

Foxtail: A soft hairbrush used for cleaning.

Fresh meat: A new nonqualified person aboard.

F.U.B.A.R.: Fucked Up Beyond All Recognition. Also known as Fouled Up Beyond All Recognition.

Gear adrift: Items not stowed away.

Geedunk: Candy, vending machine items, etc.

Gilly: Illegal pure grain alcohol. Also known as "torpedo juice."

Goat locker: A term of endearment for the chief's quarters. As in, that is where the old goats live.

Golden shellback: A sailor who crossed the International Date Line and the equator at the same point.

Gorilla snot: Compartment bulkhead stuffing tube sealer.

Growler: A sound-powered phone on older submarines.

Gun decking the logs: Filling out a form or log with mostly imaginary data. Usually done out of laziness or because the filer got behind. See also "radioing the logs" and "pencil whipping."

Halfway night: The designated night that marked the halfway point in a deployment. Usually, halfway night was marked with a special dinner and entertainment from the crew. Often in conjunction with casino night.

Hall balls: Ahead flank, or going very fast.

Hazing: The practice of a few idiots taking time-honored traditions way too far and causing injury or trauma. And sometimes people are just pussies.

"He/she made chief when Noah was a cabin boy": Refers to a very old chief. Many variations exist.

"He's/she's dumber than a box of rocks!": Self-explanatory universal phrase for a dumbass.

"He's/she's so full of crap the birds won't land on him/her!": Also self-explanatory and used for a constant bullshitter.

H.M.F.I.C.: Head Mother Fucker In Charge. Self-explanatory phrase used to designate who is in charge.

Hockey pucks: Swedish meatballs.

Hogan's alley: The berthing section of the after battery on diesel boats that doesn't have any traffic. Like a dead end street, only one way in and out.

Holidays: Mythical days of the year that are nonexistent while on deployment.

Hollywood showers: A long and normally unauthorized shower utilizing as much water as the offender wants. Normally attributed to sonar technicians and radiomen.

"Horse play leads to sick bay": Phrase meaning "don't be fucking around or you will get hurt."

Hot racking or **hot bunking**: Sharing racks. When one goes off, the other takes his place, thus the rack never gets cold. (Three men share two racks.)

"How's your wife and my kids?": Usually used by boomer sailors from opposite crews. A way of getting under their skin, but sometimes true.

"I can neither confirm nor deny the presence of nuclear weapons aboard any Navy vessel": Standard answer given to civilians when they ask whether the submarine is carrying nuclear missiles.

"I could tell you, but then I'd have to kill you": Another standard answer when a submariner is asked about specific missions they have been on.

"I had it, you got it. Any questions, I'll be in my rack": A common abbreviated, unauthorized turnover from watch stander to another. Usually used when the off-going watch stander was extremely tired.

"If it doesn't move, paint it": Poking fun at the Navy's relentless need to paint everything.

"If it's fucked—un-fuck it": In other words, if it's broken, fix it.

"If you are looking for sympathy, you can find it in the dictionary between shit and syphilis": Self-explanatory phrase used to show non-compassion.

"I'm so short, when I look in the mirror, I'm not there!": Phrase used by sailors getting close to their separation date or another important event.

"In the fan room, no one can hear you scream!": A "threat" to a non-qual who is less than motivated.

"I was never there, not aware, and have no knowledge of any particular operation": Standard reply to questions about special operations.

Joe Navy: Another term for a lifer with no life outside the Navy.

Lieu-fucking-tenant: Illustrates Navy practice of including a swear word INSIDE another word. Another favorite: abso-fucking-lutley.

Lifer: A name given to both officers and enlisted men who love the Navy and make it clear they want to be in for twenty or more years. Lifers will try to convince others to reenlist. Also, lifers say things like "there is nothing a sailor needs that is not in his sea-bag"; this usually is a comment implying that a sailor does not need to see his spouse or children.

Lifer cup: Also known as THE cup. A white porcelain coffee cup with blue stripes usually stained brown by repeated use. Never washed, except as a prank by disgruntled juniors.

"Make a hole!": Used to get people to clear a path in a cramped area. In the standard Navy, this term is meant to clear a way for a senior officer coming through. On a submarine, it's generally used to indicate that someone with a big head is trying to get through a crowd.

Mandatory fun: When attending a ship's function, such as a picnic or party, is mandatory.

M.A.R.F.: Make a Round, Fucker. Often used by missile technicians to get their roving watch to make a round through the missile compartment.

Meat gazer: A senior enlisted person who has to watch crewmembers give their urine samples all day.

Men working in the sail 1MC announcement: "There are men working in the sail. Do not raise, lower, rotate or radiate from any mast or antenna. There are men working in the sail."

Metric fuck ton: Another highly technical measuring term used when something weighs a lot. Also known as a "butt ton," "shit ton," and "that's fucking heavy."

"Mind your bubble": The indication of the ship's angle fore and aft. The Diving Officer of the Watch (DOOW, pronounced "dive") controls the angle of the ship by various means. If the angle becomes too large, he will be ordered to "mind your bubble." In rough weather near the surface, maintaining the angle on the ship can be very difficult. When the dive can no longer control the angle on the ship by the means at his disposal, he is said to have "lost the bubble."

Mouse house: Ballistic missile submarine slang description of areas usually occupied by missile technicians. Also used to describe the MCC (Missile Control Center).

Mushroom club: Imaginary club that some crew members belong to. As in "they feed us shit and keep us in the dark."

"My mood has a slight down bubble": Submarine speak for "I'm having a bad day."

Nonskid: A rough epoxy coating used for grip on the topside walking surfaces of a submarine.

No-shitter: A sea story that is mostly (never completely) fictional, and unverifiable as well. Examples: "Hey, this is a no shitter, but I once blah blah blah…" or "Hey this is a no-shitter, I got a buddy who once blah blah blah…"

N.Q.P.: Non-Qual Puke. A nonqualified crewman who is not yet able to stand watch or is not yet qualified in submarines.

N.U.B.: Non Useful Body or 'Nother Useless Body. A sailor who has not yet earned his submarine warfare qualification (dolphins).

Nut to butt: Slang used to describe packing the line in tighter.

Operation Golden Flow: Urine drug testing.

Oxy-panic: the look of terror on a shipmate's face when he is piggybacking on your EAB hose and you disconnect without warning him.

Package check: A common form of greeting where one man smacks another man's crotch. This is done not only to test the "mettle" of the one receiving the greeting, but also as a sign of camaraderie. However, ever since hazing became increasingly unpopular over the last few years, this greeting has occurred less often. Much more common in the submarine service due to the impossibility of discharge while underway.

Paper assholes: Gummed reinforcements for the page holes for a three-ring binder. A valuable commodity as manuals are constantly being used and abused and pages tend to fall out and get lost without these reinforcements.

P.A.P.E.R.C.L.I.P.: People Against People Ever Reenlisting, Civilian Life Is Preferable. Term used to show dissatisfaction with enlistment, or unity among a brotherhood of bitter and disaffected sailors, specifically submariners. Often symbolized by the wearing of a paperclip on the uniform in varying levels of prominence to indicate the sailor's level of disgruntlement.

Patrol shoes: Any type of shoe other than Navy issue that is worn underway only. Examples include tennis shoes, bowling shoes, and cowboy boots.

P.E.B.K.A.C.: Problem Exists Between Keyboard and Chair (always popular in radio and sonar). Loose interpretation: operator error.

Pecker checker: Navy doctor or corpsman.

Pencil whip: Filling out a form with mostly imaginary data. Usually done out of laziness or because the filer got behind. Also known as "gun decking" or "radioing the logs."

Periscope liberty: Viewing the outside world through a periscope. The longer you have been at sea, the better it is.

P.F.M.: Pure Fucking Magic. Normally used when something seemed to "fix itself" or an answer came about without the use of logic. Also used to describe electricity to those not familiar with the phenomenon.

Piping tab: A manual of all submarine systems (air, hydraulics, plumbing, electrical, etc.). In the older days, it was big enough to fit into your poopy suit back pocket and no non-qual was ever seen without one for fear of retribution.

Plastic cow: The dehydrated milk they use after the real milk runs out.

P.M.F.L.: Pure Mother-Fucking Luck. Usually used when skill didn't work.

Poking holes in the ocean: Underway on a submarine.

Poopy suit: Blue coveralls worn when deployed out to sea.

Portable air sample: A snipe hunt gag inflicted on "newbies." Normally, portable air samples are regularly collected by a handheld device operated by a highly qualified crewmember. In this snipe hunt gag, however, a plastic garbage bag is inflated like a balloon and sealed, sometimes with "official" forms taped to the exterior; the newbie is then dispatched to take this important atmospheric sample to the executive officer (NEVER the skipper). Depending on that particular XO's sense of humor, the newbie could possibly come back with interesting counter-orders.

Prairie chicken: Rabbit.

"Prepare to ventilate!": A phrase used to bring fresh air into the boat but more often used as a phrase after someone has let loose an obnoxious fart. Also used in conjunction with "pressure in the boat" and "crack the hatch".

Puka: Sailor-speak used to indicate a small storage location or hole.

Purging oxygen generators 1MC announcement: "The smoking lamp is out in the machinery room while purging oxygen generators." Because pure oxygen is highly explosive, it would seem that you might not want to have the "oxygen bomb" located immediately next to the only approved smoke pit on the boat, but that's how submariners roll. Luckily, we're mostly smart enough not to smoke while generating pure oxygen.

Pussy patch: A transdermal scopolamine patch for seasickness.

Rack: Bed.

Rack burn: Reddish marks seen on the face of a sailor who has just emerged from sleeping in their rack. Scorned upon if they were not supposed to be there.

Rack hound: Derogatory but usually with a hint of envy. Term used for someone who sleeps a lot. Sailor that spends more than their fair share of time in the rack. Usually spoken when seeing somebody with rack burns—"You are such a rack hound!"

Racki-dexterous: The ability to get shit out of your rack footlocker without getting out of your rack.

Racking out: Going to bed.

Radioing the logs: Filling out a form or log with mostly imaginary data. Usually done out of laziness or because the filer got behind. See also "gun decking the logs" and "pencil whipping."

Rain locker: A shower stall.

'Rats: Short for "midnight rations." Food for the midnight to 6 AM watch that usually consists of leftovers, sandwich fixings, beanie weenies, etc.

Reactor SCRAM: An inadvertent shutdown of the reactor. For coners, a completely made-up casualty developed by nucs to keep coners from having a good Hollywood shower and to secure the bug juice machine.

"Reveille, reveille, up all bunks. Drop your cocks, put on your socks, it's daylight in the swamp": Old phrase used when waking up the crew. Extinct.

Rig for red: In the old days of submarining, certain spaces in the boat would be rigged for red (all red lights) prior to going to periscope depth, when surfacing at night, or all the time in sonar. The red lights helped adjust eyes to the dark. Unfortunately, in later years studies found that the red light was irritating to the eyes and made people more aggressive. Other colors were tested and used, such as blue, yellow, and eventually low-level white (dirty gray).

Rig for sea: To get all the submarine systems lined up for sea and to ensure the boat is stowed for sea.

Rig for silent running or **ultra-quiet**: Turning off all unnecessary equipment to make the submarine as quite as possible.

Rig ship for lady visitors: Before women were allowed on submarines, the crew would be informed of women visitors so as not to say or do anything inappropriate and to put away all inappropriate locker material.

R.O.A.D. program: Retired On Active Duty. Refers to a sailor who is getting ready to retire and is not doing much more than taking up space until that time.

Roast beast: Roast beef, or any meat served aboard the ship that even the cooks who prepared it can't identify the meat.

Rock: Term used to describe a sailor who acts as though he hasn't learned anything.

Royal diamond shellback: Sailors who cross the Equator at the prime meridian.

R.T.F.M.: Read the Fucking Manual. Also known as **R.T.F.B.** (Read the Fucking Book).

R.T.F.Q.: Read the fucking question.

Sail she may, shine she must: Old sailor term used to describe the monotony of shining brass and chrome when it felt like the priorities were more to clean and shine rather than get underway to sea.

Sailor-proof: Meaning a sailor cannot break this. Unfortunately, this is much like a unicorn, the Loch Ness Monster, and Bigfoot…it has never been found. Many engineers have tried to make things sailor-proof but with only limited or no success.

Salty: Someone who has been in the Navy a long time or who has a lot of sea experience. Originates from the days of old wooden sailing ships when sailors would get covered in seawater, and upon drying, their clothes could stand on their own from all the salt.

S.C.R.A.M.: See reactor SCRAM. A term used to state that the reactor is being shut down quickly or accidentally. Many think it is an acronym for Super Critical Reactor Axe Man. In actuality, it was likely coined by the operators of the first commercial nuclear reactor. As in, "What do you do if things go wrong? You hit that big red button and scram the hell outta here!"

Screwed, blued, and tattooed: Old Navy term meant to describe what sailors did on shore leave or liberty. Screwed = self-explanatory, blued = get drunk, and tattooed = get a tattoo.

Scuttlebutt: Drinking fountain rumor (originated from the rumors that would be spread on board ship while gathered about the water barrel). Also known as "hot cock" or "the skinny."

Sea daddy: Senior, more experienced sailor who unofficially takes a new member of the crew under his wing and mentors him.

Seaman Schmuckatelli: Generic name for a sailor, used in a similar manner as "Joe Blow" or "John Q. Public." Example: "You're working on an electrical system without tagging it out, when along comes Seaman Schmuckatelli, who energizes the circuit and ZAP, you're fried calamari."

Sea pussy: A yeoman or personnel man. Akin to a secretary who does clerical work.

Sea story: Usually starts with "this is a no shitter" or "this one time in (*insert foreign port*)." It is up to the listener of the story to decide of it is true or not…kind of like these slang terms.

"Secure from field day, commence cleanup ship!": Used when cleanup during field day did not produce the desired results.

Sewer pipe sailor: Diesel submariner. Derives from the smell achieved from riding in a diesel boat.

Shaft seals: A mythological creature that lives in shaft alley. Also the mechanical device that keeps seawater from getting into the boat via the propeller shaft.

Shellback: A sailor who has crossed the equator while underway. One is only administered this title after going through a "crossing the line" ceremony where the "Court of Neptune" admits you into the brotherhood and you can shed your slimy pollywog existence. In other words, a sailor who has actually been on adventures at sea!

Sherwood Forest: Slang term used to describe the missile compartment on an SSBN submarine.

Shit on a raft: Chipped beef in gravy over toast. Also known as "shit on a shingle."

Shipmate: Any fellow Sailor. Also used as a derogatory term against all junior enlisted personnel, i.e., E-5 and below. An officer, chief or first class, will use this to show that they think so little of you, they haven't bothered to take the time out of their day to learn your name. Sometimes when used for a less-than-stellar sailor, the term "shipwreck" will be substituted.

Shit can: Either the name for a trash can or the act of throwing something into the trash.

Shit house mouse: Someone assigned to mess cook duty.

"Shit in the tanks, air in the banks, I had it you got it": A common abbreviated, unauthorized turnover from one watch stander to another. Commonly used by a chief of the watch or aux forward.

Short or short-timer: Someone with not much time left on board or in the Navy.

Shower tech: Sonar technician. They do love their showers!

Single-digit midget: A person who is down to less than ten days from getting back to port, exiting the Navy, etc.

Skate: A sailor who avoids work in general while not being detected; for example, the ability to "skate" out of work undetected while being assigned to a fourteen-man working party.

Skimmer: A derogatory term for a surface ship or a surface sailor.

Slept out: When you have slept so much that you can't sleep anymore. Not applicable to sonar technicians, radioman, and navigation electronics technicians.

Sliders: Mess deck/chow hall hamburgers/cheeseburgers, so named for their high grease content and purported ability to "slide" through the alimentary canal.

S.L.I.F.F.: Silly Little Ignorant Fat Fuck.

"Smile! At least your wife is getting laid": A fun term used by qualified personnel to nonqualified personnel. Normally more effective the longer a non-qualification person has gone without a family-gram.

Smoking lamp: A term used to designate a place or time when smoking is allowed. Becoming extinct.

Smoke test: Slang for testing something at full power or turning on a piece of damaged equipment.

S.N.A.F.U.: Situation Normal All Fucked Up or Situation Normal All Fouled Up.

S.N.O.B.: Shortest Nuc On Board. The nuclear-qualified person with the least amount of time left in the Navy on their initial enlistment. Reenlisters do not qualify.

"So, what are they going to do? Take my birthday away?": Many variations of this phrase exist, such as "So, what are they going to do? Ship me out on a fast attack?" and "So, what are they going to do? Send me to sea?" Used as a form of rebellion.

Spin up all missiles: To make ballistic missiles ready for launch.

S.S.N.: Saturdays, Sundays, and Nights. In reference to SSN (fast attack) submarines working seven days a week. Actual abbreviation is for Sub-Surface Nuclear.

Steel beach picnic: Celebration on the topside of a submarine usually involving a swim call and barbecue.

Steely-eyed stealthy killers of the deep: Submarine sailors.

Still: Evaporator.

Submarine shower: A shower consisting of turning on the shower for a few seconds to wet down, turning off the shower to lather up, and turning on the shower again for a few seconds to rinse off. Used to conserve water.

Sucking rubber: Wearing an EAB.

"Suffers from dietary indiscretion": Describing an overweight sailor.

S.W.A.G.: Sophisticated Wild Ass Guess or Some Wild Ass Guess. See also EWAG.

Sweat pumps: When someone is worrying too much and they are always running at full speed. An excitable person, or one who takes humorous situations too seriously. "Their sweat pumps are at high speed!"

System heavy: A submariner who is known for his extensive knowledge of certain submarine systems.

System light: A submariner who is known for his less than extensive knowledge of certain submarine systems. Often sought out by non-quals who are delinquent or trying to skate by.

Tacking on dolphins: "Extinct" tradition of punching a newly qualified submariner's dolphins onto their chest. Unfortunately, some got carried away and punched too hard, causing injury and making the act a hazing incident. Tacking on dolphins is considered taboo in today's submarine force.

"Take her down, take her deep, damn the pressure, damn the heat, make your depth 500 feet!": Unauthorized poetic command to submerge the ship or change to a deeper depth.

"Take her up to broach depth": Unauthorized phrase said to a diving officer who has a reputation for broaching the submarine (breaking the surface of the ocean with the hull) and thus exposing the boat to detection, or when the weather and sea state are extremely bad and broaching is expected.

"Taking a suction on the boat": Used to describe what a FLOB is doing.

Target: Term to describe any ship or boat on the surface.

TDU it: Trash Disposal Unit. To throw something in the trash. Also known as deep-sixing in the surface Navy. Sometimes pronounced "tadooing it."

Ten punches in the hacker card: A hacker card is for submariners who sit through extremely bad movies. The number of punches indicates how bad the movie was rated.

"There's air in the banks, shit in the tanks…don't worry about the fire, the flooding will put it out": Another abbreviated, humorous, unauthorized way of giving an off-going watch relief.

The cup: See "lifer cup."

"There ain't no slack in a fast attack": Used in reference to the heavy sea time schedule fast attack sailors keep and their thought that they do the job better than everyone else.

The skinny: The latest news or rumors. Also known as "hot cock" or "scuttlebutt."

"This page intentionally left blank": Written into manual and log pages that were intentionally left blank, usually indicating the last page of a chapter or section.

Tits up: Broke-dick, inoperable, dead (from some piece of equipment being "flat on its back"). Sometimes referred to as "tango uniform."

T.L.D.: Thermo-Luminescent Dosimeter, used to determine exposure to radiation.

Top secret shellback: Submariners who have crossed the equator at a classified degree of longitude.

Torpedo man's tweaker: A very large wrench.

"Train like you fight, fight like you train": Most common submarine phrase found on a poster in just about any training building.

Trim party: A prank often perpetrated on a newly qualified dive officer or chief of the watch, where men and other weights are shifted fore and aft to affect the trim of the boat.

T.S.T.C.: Too Short To Care.

Turd Chaser: Slang term for an A-ganger, because they work on plumbing systems.

Turn to: Get started.

Tweaker: Electronics ratings; any engineering rating not turning a wrench. Rates such as ET, RM, FT, and ST who "tweak" electronic components to make them work again. The term is also used to describe a very small screwdriver.

Tweener: Affectionate term for missile technicians on ballistic missile submarines. Usually called out during the "coner" and "nuc" throwbacks, since the missile compartment is "between" the forward (coner) and engineering (nuc) spaces.

Twidget: Sailor in the electronics or electrical fields of job specialties.

Two-fisted gagger: Used to describe an incredibly bad movie.

Typewriter repair man: Cryptological technician, spook, or special operations rider.

Ustafish: Pronounced "used-ta-fish." General term for a previous submarine command. Often used as "That's not how we did it aboard the ustafish." Generally followed by various short, forceful comments from others present.

Water slug: Refers to shooting a submarine's torpedo tube without first loading a torpedo. Often used as a joke to play on new non-quals. Shooting a water slug usually results in the shooter getting to clean out the torpedo tube.

W.E.T.S.U.: We Eat This Shit Up. A derisive statement, usually regarding working or living conditions.

"Won't rust, bust, or take on dust": An equipment or tool that is damn-near sailor-proof.

W.T.F.O.: What the Fuck, Over?

Zoomies: Radiation.

Zulu 5 Oscar: Personnel making a deliberate attempt to board a ship unauthorized, usually at the direction of higher authority to test security procedures. The standard intruder drill.

Bibliography

Adams, JOC Cindy. 2017. *USS Tang Survivors.* 05 09. http://ss563.org/306/survivors.html.

American Marketing Association. 2013. *About AMA.* July. Accessed May 15, 2017. https://www.ama.org/AboutAMA/Pages/Definition-of-Marketing.aspx.

Campbell, Rick. 2017. *Welcome to Submarine 101!* Accessed May 18, 2017. http://rickcampbellauthor.com/styled/index.html.

Dictionary.com. n.d. *Advertising.* Accessed May 15, 2017. http://www.dictionary.com/browse/advertising.

Ferriss, Tim. 2006. *4-Hour Work Week.* New York: Crown Publishing Group.

Hill, Napoleon. 1937. *Think and Grow Rich.* Meriden, CT: Ralston Society.

Kennedy, Dan S. 2006. *The Ultimate Sales Letter.* Edited by 3rd. Avon, MA: Adams Media.

Wikipedia. 2017. *Nuclear Marine Propulsion.* Accessed May 18, 2017. https://en.wikipedia.org/wiki/Nuclear_marine_propulsion.

Womack, James P. 2002. *Lean Thinking.* New York: Simon and Schuster.

About the Author

As a U.S. Navy submariner, Jeff Barnes traveled the world underwater at extreme depths, running a nuclear power plant and sleeping with torpedoes while learning invaluable skills. His innate leadership ability and understanding of complex systems allowed him to run the largest division on his submarine and take charge of the ship's quality control program.

After an honorable discharge from the Navy, Jeff took his expertise and experience to corporate America, helping clients grow their businesses as a risk management consultant while also coaching and consulting small business owners on the side.

This led to Jeff running his own division inside a Fortune 500 company focused on technology and innovation, leading multiple international innovation projects and bringing new products and services to the global market. As a result of this exposure, Jeff has given training to thousands of executives on how to utilize technology and innovation to grow a business.

As an entrepreneur himself and a best-selling author, Jeff has trained, coached, and consulted with hundreds of entrepreneurs and business owners to implement complex growth systems to help them grow their companies quickly and make a positive impact on the world.

This led to Jeff becoming the CEO for Angel Investors Network, an organization helping entrepreneurs achieve their dreams since 1997. In this role he works with A-list business executives and celebrities such as Steve Forbes of Forbes Media, Kevin Harrington from ABC's Shark Tank, the co-founder of Whole Foods John Mackey, and many others. Jeff continues helping entrepreneurs find the investors and funding they need to scale their businesses fast, and acts as a preliminary judge on Angel Investors Network's "Pitch Tank" – a live Shark Tank style event hosted in front of thousands of investors (www.ThePitchTank.com).

Jeff spends a great deal of time coaching his two boys' sports teams and traveling. Jeff continues traveling the world speaking and finding great places for scuba diving, a skill he gained as a former U.S. Navy scuba diver. Jeff's love for the outdoors, camping, diving, the environment and helping others earned him a seat on the board of Lifeschool, a nonprofit organization helping under-privileged youth gain skills they don't learn in school.

The Most Amazing Opportunity You'll Get Today!

Get it All for Just $1!

This book, although amazing and fun (in my humble opinion), is not complete without the accompanying resources in store for you online. I have taken the time to provide you with additional tools, resources, work books, and even some audio interviews I've conducted with others over the years to help you scale your business faster and with greater certainty.

The goal of this book and its bonuses is to help you scale your business using the right strategies coupled with the right systems, allowing you to make a greater positive impact in this world. By purchasing this book, whether the e-book, audiobook, or physical print copy, you are entitled to receive all these incredible resources **for just $1** by simply visiting the webpage listed below.

It is my sincere hope that you will take me up on this offer and grab your resources today. After all, some of the strategies listed inside these two covers could get me blacklisted and the website shut down![*] So be sure to grab your bonuses today!

Since this book was first released, I took over the role of CEO at Angel Investors Network and have moved all of our resources over there. Now you can access our Inner Circle and get access to over 100 hours of additional training on how to start, scale, and eventually sell or exit your business.

At Angel Investors Network we are helping you create wealth and abundance through the power of Angel Investing & Entrepreneurship.

---

[*] Okay, maybe they won't get me shut down, but you never know!

All Hands on Deck is a great complement to the resources we have available online, and now you can access everything starting at just one dollar!

To get access to these incredible resources, including live training, workbooks, and more, simply visit www.AngelNetwork.com/Bonus.

Go to www.AngelNetwork.com/Bonus to get started today!

www.ingramcontent.com/pod-product-compliance
Lightning Source LLC
Chambersburg PA
CBHW052312220526
45472CB00001B/85